Mastering Veterinary Skills

Essential Training for Aspiring Animal Care Experts

Emily Kelley

The presentation of the information is without contract or any type of guarantee assurance. The trademarks that are used are without any consent, and the publication of the trademark is without permission or backing by the trademark owner. All trademarks and brands within this book are for clarifying purposes only and are the owned by the owners themselves, not affiliated with this document.

Table of Contents

Chapter 1

Introduction

The Journey into Veterinary Medicine

Embarking on the journey into veterinary medicine is akin to setting out on an expedition filled with discovery, challenges, and profound purpose. The path is often marked by a deep-seated passion for animals and a desire to alleviate suffering, coupled with the intellectual rigor required to master the biological sciences. For many, this journey begins with a childhood fascination—perhaps the awe-inspiring sight of a veterinarian caring for a beloved pet or a fascination with the myriad creatures that inhabit our world. Yet, beyond the initial spark of interest lies a complex and demanding field that requires unwavering dedication and a commitment to lifelong learning.

Aspiring veterinarians quickly discover that their path is not just about acquiring technical skills but also about cultivating a mindset of empathy and resilience. The road to becoming a veterinary professional involves rigorous academic training, practical experience, and the development of a nuanced understanding of the ethical dimensions of animal care. This journey demands an ability to navigate the delicate balance between science and compassion, where clinical decisions are informed by both data and the well-being of the patient.

In the early stages of this journey, students immerse themselves in the foundational sciences that form the bedrock of veterinary medicine. Courses in biology, chemistry, and physics lay the groundwork for understanding the complexities of animal physiology and pathology. These subjects, while challenging, are essential for developing the analytical skills needed to diagnose and treat a diverse range of species. The classroom becomes a crucible where future veterinarians hone their capacity for critical thinking and problem-solving, preparing them for the dynamic and unpredictable nature of clinical practice.

Beyond the classroom, hands-on experience is a crucial component of veterinary training. Aspiring veterinarians are encouraged to seek opportunities for practical learning, whether through internships, volunteer work, or part-time employment in veterinary clinics or animal shelters. These experiences provide invaluable insights into the day-to-day realities of veterinary practice, from conducting routine health checks to managing complex medical cases. Working alongside experienced practitioners allows students to observe the art of veterinary medicine in action, witnessing firsthand the delicate dance between diagnosis and treatment.

The journey into veterinary medicine is also deeply intertwined with the development of interpersonal skills. Effective communication is paramount, as veterinarians must convey complex medical information to pet owners, collaborate with colleagues, and advocate for animal welfare. The ability to build trust and rapport with clients is as critical as technical competence, for it is through these relationships that veterinarians can truly make a difference in the lives of animals and their human companions. This aspect of the profession requires emotional intelligence and the ability to navigate the nuances of human-animal relationships.

As students progress through their training, they are introduced to the diverse specialties within veterinary medicine. From small animal practice to equine health, wildlife conservation, and exotic animal care, the field offers a plethora of avenues for exploration and specialization. Each area presents its own unique challenges and rewards, allowing veterinarians to align their careers with their individual interests and passions. The choice of specialization often reflects a personal connection to a particular species or an interest in addressing specific health challenges, such as infectious diseases, surgery, or nutrition.

Ethical considerations form a critical component of the veterinary journey, prompting future veterinarians to reflect on the broader implications of their work. The responsibility of caring for sentient beings requires a commitment to ethical practice, where decisions are guided by principles of animal welfare and respect for life. Veterinarians must grapple with complex ethical dilemmas, such as balancing the needs of individual animals with those of their human caretakers or addressing the challenges of overpopulation and limited resources. These considerations underscore the importance of developing a strong moral compass and the ability to make informed, compassionate decisions.

Throughout this journey, the importance of mentorship cannot be overstated. Seasoned veterinarians serve as guides and role models, offering support, encouragement, and wisdom to those embarking on their careers. Mentorship provides a safe space for aspiring veterinarians to seek advice, ask questions, and learn from the experiences of others. It fosters a sense of community and shared purpose, reinforcing the values and ideals that underpin the profession.

The Importance of Mastery in Veterinary Skills

Mastering veterinary skills is a cornerstone of effective animal care, bridging the gap between theoretical knowledge and practical application. The pursuit of mastery in this field is not merely about acquiring technical proficiency; it encompasses a holistic approach that integrates empathy, critical thinking, and a lifelong commitment to learning. For aspiring veterinarians, achieving mastery is a journey that demands dedication, perseverance, and an unwavering passion for animal welfare.

In the world of veterinary medicine, the stakes are high. Animals rely on veterinarians to diagnose, treat, and prevent illnesses, often without the ability to communicate their symptoms. This unique challenge requires a deep understanding of animal physiology and behavior, coupled with the ability to interpret subtle cues that indicate distress or discomfort. Mastery in veterinary skills involves honing one's observational abilities, developing an intuitive sense of animal health, and cultivating the patience to listen to what is often unsaid.

Technical expertise is undoubtedly a vital component of veterinary mastery. From performing delicate surgical procedures to administering life-saving medications, veterinarians must possess a comprehensive understanding of anatomy, pharmacology, and medical techniques. This expertise is built through years of rigorous training, hands-on experience, and continuous education. However, true mastery extends beyond technical skills, encompassing the ability to adapt to new challenges and embrace emerging technologies that enhance diagnostic and treatment capabilities.

An essential aspect of achieving mastery in veterinary skills is the development of problem-solving abilities. Animals present with a wide range of medical conditions, each requiring a tailored approach to diagnosis and treatment. Veterinarians must possess the analytical skills to assess complex cases, synthesize information from various sources, and formulate effective treatment plans. This process often involves collaboration with colleagues, consultation with specialists, and a willingness to explore unconventional solutions when traditional methods fall short.

Mastery in veterinary skills also requires a profound commitment to ethical practice. Veterinarians are entrusted with the responsibility of making decisions that impact the lives of animals and their human caretakers. This responsibility necessitates a strong moral compass, guiding practitioners to prioritize animal welfare while balancing the needs and expectations of clients. Ethical dilemmas are an inherent part of veterinary practice, challenging veterinarians to navigate complex situations with compassion, integrity, and professionalism.

Communication is another critical skill that underpins veterinary mastery. Veterinarians must effectively convey complex medical information to clients, ensuring that pet owners understand the nature of their animal's condition and the rationale behind recommended treatments. This requires clarity, empathy, and the ability to tailor communication styles to suit diverse audiences. Building strong relationships with clients fosters trust and collaboration, empowering pet owners to make informed decisions about their animal's care.

The journey to mastery is a continual process of growth and development. Veterinary medicine is a dynamic field, characterized by rapid advancements in research, technology, and treatment modalities. To remain at the forefront of the profession, veterinarians must embrace a mindset of lifelong learning, staying abreast of the latest developments and refining their skills through ongoing education and professional development. This commitment to learning ensures that veterinarians are equipped to provide the highest standard of care, ultimately improving outcomes for their patients.

Beyond the clinical setting, mastery in veterinary skills involves engagement with the broader community. Veterinarians play a vital role in public health, wildlife conservation, and animal advocacy. By participating in outreach programs, contributing to research initiatives, and advocating for animal welfare policies, veterinarians extend their impact beyond individual patients to influence systemic change. This broader perspective enriches the practice of veterinary medicine, fostering a sense of purpose and fulfillment that transcends the confines of the clinic.

For aspiring veterinarians, the pursuit of mastery is both a challenge and an opportunity. It demands resilience in the face of setbacks, a willingness to learn from mistakes, and the courage to push beyond one's comfort zone. While the path is demanding, the rewards are immeasurable. Mastery in veterinary skills enables practitioners to make a tangible difference in the lives of animals and their caretakers, contributing to a world where animals receive the compassion, respect, and care they deserve.

In the quest for mastery, mentorship emerges as a powerful catalyst for growth. Experienced veterinarians serve as guides and mentors, offering invaluable insights, support, and encouragement to those embarking on their careers. Mentorship provides a platform for learning, reflection, and shared experiences, creating a nurturing environment where aspiring veterinarians can flourish. This sense of community reinforces the values and ideals that underpin the profession, inspiring the next generation of veterinarians to strive for excellence.

How This Book Will Guide Your Path

Embarking on a journey into the world of veterinary medicine is a transformative experience, one that is deeply personal yet universally challenging. This book is designed to be your trusted companion as you navigate this path, offering guidance, insights, and practical advice to support your growth and development as an aspiring animal care expert. Whether you are just beginning your journey or seeking to deepen your expertise, the content within these pages is crafted to provide a comprehensive roadmap that addresses the diverse facets of veterinary practice.

The field of veterinary medicine is vast and multifaceted, encompassing a wide range of disciplines, each with its own unique challenges and rewards. This book is structured to reflect this diversity, offering a holistic perspective that integrates foundational knowledge, technical skills, and ethical considerations. By immersing yourself in these chapters, you will gain a deeper understanding of the core principles that underlie veterinary practice, while also exploring the nuances that differentiate various specialties.

One of the key ways this book will guide your path is by providing a solid foundation in the essential sciences that form the backbone of veterinary medicine. Understanding the evolution of veterinary science and the intricacies of anatomy and physiology is crucial for developing the analytical skills needed to diagnose and treat a wide array of species. By delving into these foundational topics, you will build a strong framework that supports your ability to make informed clinical decisions.

In addition to scientific knowledge, this book emphasizes the importance of understanding animal behavior and communication. Animals are sentient beings with complex emotional and social needs, and recognizing these aspects is vital for providing compassionate and effective care. Through the exploration of veterinary terminology and the nuances of animal behavior, you will be equipped to interpret the subtle cues that are essential for accurate diagnosis and treatment.

As you progress through the book, you will encounter in-depth discussions on diagnostic techniques and tools. The ability to accurately assess an animal's health is a cornerstone of veterinary practice, and this book provides a detailed overview of the various methods used to gather and interpret diagnostic data. From physical examinations to advanced imaging technologies, you will gain insight into the tools and techniques that enable veterinarians to deliver precise and effective care.

The book also addresses the critical area of medical treatments and procedures, offering practical guidance on pharmacology, emergency care, and pain management. These sections are designed to provide you with the knowledge and skills needed to administer treatments safely and effectively, ensuring the best possible outcomes for your patients. By exploring both conventional and alternative approaches to veterinary medicine, you will be empowered to make holistic and informed decisions tailored to each animal's unique needs.

Surgical skills and techniques are another focal point of this book, highlighting the importance of precision, safety, and innovation in veterinary surgery. The chapters dedicated to this topic provide a comprehensive overview of surgical preparation, procedures, and post-operative care, equipping you with the tools needed to navigate the complexities of surgical practice. By understanding the principles of sterilization, safety, and recovery, you will be prepared to manage surgical cases with confidence and competence.

Recognizing the integral role of nutrition in animal health, this book delves into the intricacies of animal nutrition and well-being. Proper nutrition is fundamental to disease prevention and recovery, and this book offers detailed insights into the nutritional needs of different species. By evaluating commercial and homemade diets, you will be able to develop tailored nutritional plans that promote optimal health and well-being for your patients.

The exploration of specialized veterinary fields offers a glimpse into the diverse career paths available within the profession. From wildlife medicine to equine health and small animal practice, this book introduces you to the unique challenges and opportunities associated with each specialty. By understanding the distinct requirements and considerations of these fields, you will be better positioned to pursue a career that aligns with your interests and passions.

Ethics and professionalism are woven throughout the book, underscoring the importance of ethical decision-making and professional conduct in veterinary practice. As you navigate the complexities of animal care, you will encounter ethical dilemmas that require careful consideration and reflection. This book provides guidance on navigating these challenges with integrity and compassion, ensuring that your practice is grounded in principles of respect and responsibility.

Chapter 2

Foundations of Veterinary Medicine

Evolution of Veterinary Science

The origins of veterinary science trace back to the ancient world, where the well-being of animals was intrinsically linked to human survival and prosperity. Early records from Egypt, Mesopotamia, and the Indus Valley reveal the existence of primitive veterinary practices, often intertwined with religious rituals and folklore. These early practitioners, though lacking the scientific knowledge we possess today, recognized the importance of animal health, not only for agricultural productivity but also for companionship and transportation. They laid the groundwork for a field that would evolve dramatically over the millennia, shaped by cultural, scientific, and technological advancements.

The formalization of veterinary science began in earnest during the Greco-Roman era, where notable figures such as Hippocrates and Aristotle made significant contributions to the understanding of animal anatomy and disease. Their observations and writings provided a rudimentary framework for veterinary medicine, emphasizing the connection between human and animal health. However, it was not until the Middle Ages that more systematic approaches to animal care emerged, largely driven by the demands of the burgeoning horse and livestock industries in Europe and the Middle East.

The establishment of the first veterinary school in Lyon, France, in 1761 marked a pivotal moment in the evolution of veterinary science. Founded by Claude Bourgelat, the school represented a shift towards a more structured and scientific approach to animal health, emphasizing empirical observation, anatomical dissection, and disease classification. This institution set the stage for the professionalization of veterinary medicine, inspiring the creation of similar schools across Europe and beyond.

The 19th century witnessed significant advancements in veterinary science, spurred by the broader scientific revolution and increased global exploration. The development of germ theory by pioneers like Louis Pasteur and Robert Koch transformed the understanding of infectious diseases, leading to breakthroughs in vaccination and disease prevention. These discoveries had profound implications for veterinary practice, enabling more effective control of zoonotic diseases and supporting the health of both animals and humans.

As veterinary science progressed into the 20th century, the focus expanded beyond disease treatment to encompass animal welfare, nutrition, and behavior. The rise of the pet industry, coupled with growing awareness of animal rights, prompted a shift towards more holistic and compassionate approaches to veterinary care. This period also saw the integration of advanced technologies, such as radiography and ultrasound, which revolutionized diagnostic capabilities and improved treatment outcomes.

The latter half of the 20th century and the early 21st century have been characterized by rapid technological and scientific advancements that continue to reshape veterinary science. The advent of molecular biology and genetics has opened new frontiers in disease research and treatment, enabling personalized medicine and targeted therapies. Innovations in digital technology and telemedicine have expanded access to veterinary care, providing new tools for monitoring animal health and enhancing communication between veterinarians and clients.

One of the most significant developments in recent years has been the growing recognition of the interconnectedness of human, animal, and environmental health—a concept known as One Health. This holistic approach emphasizes the need for collaborative efforts across disciplines to address global health challenges, such as emerging infectious diseases, food security, and biodiversity conservation. Veterinary science plays a crucial role in these initiatives, contributing valuable insights and expertise to promote the health and well-being of all species.

The evolution of veterinary science is also marked by an increasing emphasis on ethical considerations and professional responsibility. As society's relationship with animals continues to evolve, veterinarians are called upon to navigate complex ethical dilemmas, balancing the needs of individual animals with broader societal and environmental concerns. This requires a commitment to ongoing education, reflection, and dialogue, ensuring that veterinary practice aligns with evolving ethical standards and societal values.

Looking to the future, the field of veterinary science is poised for continued growth and innovation. Advances in artificial intelligence, biotechnology, and data analytics hold the potential to revolutionize veterinary care, offering new solutions for disease prevention, diagnosis, and treatment. As these technologies become increasingly integrated into practice, veterinarians will need to adapt and embrace new skills, ensuring that they remain at the forefront of animal health care.

Moreover, the global nature of contemporary veterinary challenges demands a collaborative and interdisciplinary approach. Veterinary professionals will play a critical role in addressing pressing issues such as climate change, antimicrobial resistance, and wildlife conservation. By working alongside experts from other fields, veterinarians can contribute to the development of sustainable solutions that benefit both animals and humans.

Essential Anatomy and Physiology

Understanding the intricate tapestry of animal anatomy and physiology is fundamental for any aspiring veterinarian. These two interconnected fields provide the blueprint for comprehending how animals function, offering essential insights into their health and well-being. Mastering these subjects is akin to learning a new language, one that allows you to interpret the silent narratives of your patients and respond effectively to their needs.

Anatomy, the study of the structure of living organisms, serves as the foundation for understanding the complex architecture of animal bodies. From the smallest rodent to the largest whale, each species boasts a unique anatomical design tailored to its environment and lifestyle. This diversity is not only fascinating but also critical for veterinary practice, as it requires customized approaches to diagnosis and treatment. As you delve into the study of anatomy, you'll encounter a rich tapestry of systems, each with its own distinct role in maintaining life.

The skeletal system provides the structural framework for the body, offering support and protection for vital organs. It is essential to recognize the variations in skeletal structures across different species, as these differences influence mobility, posture, and susceptibility to injury. The avian skeleton, for instance, is lightweight and optimized for flight, while the robust skeletal structure of a horse is designed to bear significant weight and facilitate powerful locomotion. Understanding these variations allows veterinarians to tailor their care to the specific needs of each animal.

In tandem with the skeletal system, the muscular system enables movement and stability. Muscles work in concert with bones to produce motion, and their health is crucial for an animal's overall well-being. Veterinary professionals must be adept at identifying muscular disorders and injuries, ranging from strains and sprains to more complex conditions like myopathies. A thorough understanding of muscle anatomy and function is essential for devising effective rehabilitation and treatment plans.

The circulatory system, comprised of the heart, blood vessels, and blood, is responsible for transporting nutrients, oxygen, and waste products throughout the body. This system is vital for maintaining homeostasis and supporting cellular function. Veterinarians must be proficient in assessing cardiovascular health, using techniques such as auscultation, palpation, and diagnostic imaging to identify conditions like heart murmurs, arrhythmias, and vascular diseases. A strong grasp of circulatory anatomy and physiology is essential for diagnosing and managing these conditions.

Respiratory anatomy and physiology are equally critical, as they underpin the processes of gas exchange and oxygen delivery. The respiratory system is tasked with bringing oxygen into the body and expelling carbon dioxide, a byproduct of metabolism. Understanding the mechanics of breathing, from the nasal passages to the alveoli, enables veterinarians to assess respiratory function and address conditions such as asthma, pneumonia, and tracheal collapse. Familiarity with species-specific respiratory adaptations, such as the air sacs in birds or the elongated trachea of giraffes, is crucial for accurate diagnosis and treatment.

The digestive system, responsible for nutrient absorption and waste elimination, is another key area of focus. Each species has evolved a digestive system suited to its diet and lifestyle, from the complex ruminant stomach of cattle to the simple monogastric system of dogs and cats. Veterinary professionals must understand these anatomical and physiological differences to effectively manage gastrointestinal health and address issues like malabsorption, colic, and dietary intolerances.

The nervous system, a complex network of neurons and synapses, orchestrates the body's responses to internal and external stimuli. This system is integral to sensation, movement, and cognition, making it a focal point for veterinary care. Neurological examinations and diagnostic tests help veterinarians identify conditions such as epilepsy, neuropathies, and spinal cord injuries. A comprehensive understanding of nervous system anatomy and physiology is essential for developing effective treatment strategies and improving quality of life for affected animals.

The endocrine system, composed of glands that secrete hormones, regulates numerous physiological processes, including growth, metabolism, and reproduction. Hormonal imbalances can lead to a range of health issues, from diabetes and thyroid disorders to reproductive challenges. Veterinary professionals must be well-versed in endocrine anatomy and physiology to diagnose and manage these conditions, utilizing tools such as blood tests, imaging, and hormone assays.

The integumentary system, encompassing the skin, hair, and nails, serves as the body's first line of defense against environmental threats. This system plays a crucial role in thermoregulation, hydration, and protection from pathogens. Veterinarians must be skilled in identifying skin disorders, parasites, and injuries, employing techniques such as dermatological examinations and biopsies to diagnose and treat these conditions.

Understanding Animal Behavior

In the vast and dynamic world of veterinary medicine, understanding animal behavior is a crucial skill that bridges the gap between human caregivers and their non-verbal companions. Every animal, whether a purring cat, a loyal dog, a majestic horse, or an exotic bird, communicates its needs, emotions, and intentions through behavior. For veterinarians, deciphering these behavioral cues is essential for accurate diagnosis, effective treatment, and ensuring the welfare of their patients.

Animal behavior is a rich tapestry woven from genetics, environment, and individual experiences. It encompasses everything from instinctual actions to learned responses, and it varies significantly across species, breeds, and even individual animals. For beginners in veterinary practice, the ability to interpret these behaviors begins with keen observation and an open mind. It's about becoming attuned to the subtle signals animals use to express themselves and recognizing patterns that may indicate underlying health issues.

One of the most fundamental aspects of understanding animal behavior is recognizing normal versus abnormal actions. Normal behavior varies greatly depending on the species. For instance, a rabbit's natural inclination to chew is perfectly healthy, while a dog's obsessive biting might signal anxiety or discomfort. Similarly, birds preen to maintain their feathers, but excessive feather plucking could indicate stress. By establishing a baseline of what constitutes normal behavior for different species, veterinarians can more easily identify deviations that may warrant further investigation.

Communication is at the heart of animal behavior, and it manifests in various forms, including vocalizations, body language, and scent. Dogs, for example, use a combination of barking, tail wagging, and postures to convey their feelings. A wagging tail might suggest excitement, but if accompanied by a lowered body and tucked ears, it could indicate fear. Similarly, cats might purr when content, but a persistent, loud purr can sometimes signal pain or distress. Horses, with their expressive eyes and ears, communicate a wide range of emotions, from relaxation to agitation. Understanding these signals allows veterinarians to assess the emotional state of their patients and adapt their approach accordingly.

The environment plays a significant role in shaping animal behavior. Factors such as space, social interactions, and stimuli can profoundly impact how animals behave. For instance, an overcrowded living space might lead to aggression in typically docile animals, while isolation can cause withdrawal or depression. Veterinarians must consider the environmental context when evaluating behavior, as changes or stressors in an animal's surroundings often manifest in their actions. Conducting thorough environmental assessments and obtaining comprehensive histories from owners can provide valuable insights into behavioral issues.

Social structures and hierarchies also influence animal behavior. Many animals, particularly those that naturally live in groups, have complex social systems that dictate interactions. In dogs, for example, understanding pack dynamics can help explain behaviors like dominance or submission. Similarly, horses establish pecking orders within their herds, which can affect how they interact with other horses and humans. Recognizing these social cues is crucial for veterinarians, as it helps inform treatment plans and behavioral interventions.

Behavioral problems are a common concern among pet owners, and veterinarians play a pivotal role in addressing these issues. Whether it's a barking dog, a scratching cat, or a parrot that screams incessantly, these behaviors often stem from unmet needs, anxiety, or medical conditions. Veterinarians must employ a multifaceted approach to diagnosing and treating behavioral problems, combining medical evaluations with behavioral assessments. Identifying the root cause of a behavior is key, whether it's a health issue, environmental factor, or learned habit.

Training and behavioral modification are effective tools for managing and improving animal behavior. Positive reinforcement, where desirable behaviors are rewarded, is a widely accepted method that encourages learning and adaptation without causing fear or stress. Veterinarians often collaborate with trainers and behaviorists to develop personalized training programs that address specific behavioral challenges. Educating pet owners about the principles of positive reinforcement and consistent training can foster harmonious relationships between animals and their caregivers.

Ethology, the scientific study of animal behavior, provides valuable insights into why animals act the way they do. By observing animals in their natural environments, ethologists have uncovered patterns and behaviors that are deeply ingrained in an animal's biology. This knowledge helps veterinarians understand behaviors that may seem perplexing in a domestic setting but are perfectly normal in the wild. For example, a cat's tendency to hunt and stalk, even when well-fed, is a remnant of its predatory instincts. Appreciating these natural behaviors allows veterinarians to offer informed advice to pet owners on managing such instincts in a domestic environment.

The bond between animals and humans is a unique and powerful influence on behavior. Animals often mirror the emotions and stress levels of their human companions, leading to behavioral changes. A stressed or anxious owner can inadvertently transfer those emotions to their pet, resulting in similar behaviors. Veterinarians must be sensitive to the dynamics of the human-animal bond, as strengthening this relationship can lead to significant improvements in behavior and overall well-being.

Veterinary Terminology 101

Navigating the world of veterinary medicine requires fluency in a specialized language that may initially seem daunting to those new to the field. Veterinary terminology, much like any other professional lexicon, serves as a precise and efficient means of communication among practitioners. It is a tool that transforms complex medical concepts into understandable dialogue, facilitating the accurate exchange of information critical to animal care. Gaining a solid grasp of this terminology is an essential step for anyone embarking on a journey in veterinary medicine.

At the heart of veterinary terminology lies a foundation of root words, prefixes, and suffixes, predominantly derived from Latin and Greek. Understanding these components allows for the construction and deconstruction of complex terms, offering insights into their meanings. For instance, the term "gastroenteritis" can be broken down into "gastro-" meaning stomach, "enter-" meaning intestine, and "-itis" indicating inflammation. Thus, "gastroenteritis" refers to inflammation of the stomach and intestines. This systematic approach to terminology enables practitioners to decipher unfamiliar words and enhances their ability to communicate effectively.

One of the primary areas of focus in veterinary terminology is anatomy, as it provides the vocabulary needed to describe the structure and function of animal bodies. Familiarity with anatomical terms is crucial for accurately locating and discussing specific body parts and systems. Terms such as "cranial" (toward the head), "caudal" (toward the tail), "dorsal" (the back), and "ventral" (the belly) are fundamental descriptors used in physical examinations and medical documentation. Mastery of these directional terms ensures clarity and precision when referring to anatomical locations.

Beyond basic anatomical terminology, understanding terms related to body systems is paramount. Each system, from the cardiovascular to the integumentary, has its own set of specialized vocabulary. For example, terms like "myocardium" (heart muscle) and "endocarditis" (inflammation of the inner lining of the heart) are essential for discussing cardiac health. Similarly, "dermatophyte" (a fungus affecting the skin) and "alopecia" (hair loss) are common terms within the context of dermatology. A comprehensive understanding of system-specific vocabulary supports accurate diagnosis and effective communication with colleagues and clients.

Veterinary terminology also encompasses the language of diagnostics and treatment. Terms such as "radiography" (imaging using X-rays), "biopsy" (removal of tissue for examination), and "anesthesia" (induced loss of sensation) are integral to describing medical procedures and interventions. Knowledge of these terms is essential for developing treatment plans, documenting patient care, and communicating with pet owners in a way that is both informative and reassuring.

Pharmacology, the study of drugs and their effects, is another critical area of veterinary terminology. Understanding drug classifications, such as "antibiotics" (agents that kill or inhibit bacteria) and "analgesics" (pain relievers), is vital for prescribing and administering medications safely. Additionally, terms like "dosage" (the amount of medication given) and "contraindication" (a reason to withhold a treatment) are crucial for ensuring the efficacy and safety of pharmacological interventions.

While veterinary terminology is a powerful tool for communication, it is equally important to convey complex medical information in a manner that is accessible to clients. Pet owners may not be familiar with technical jargon, so veterinarians must be adept at translating terminology into layman's terms without compromising the accuracy of the information. This skill fosters trust and collaboration, empowering clients to make informed decisions about their animal's care.

To aid in the mastery of veterinary terminology, many practitioners rely on mnemonics and visual aids. Mnemonics, or memory aids, can simplify the learning process by associating complex terms with familiar concepts. For instance, remembering the phrase "Old People From Texas Eat Spiders" can help recall the cranial nerves: olfactory, optic, oculomotor, trochlear, trigeminal, abducens, and facial. Visual aids, such as anatomical diagrams and charts, provide a visual reference that reinforces understanding and retention of terminology.

Consistent practice and immersion in the language of veterinary medicine are key to becoming proficient in terminology. Engaging with veterinary literature, attending seminars, and participating in clinical experiences offer opportunities to encounter and apply terminology in real-world contexts. Collaborating with mentors and peers also provides valuable feedback and reinforcement, helping solidify one's understanding of veterinary vocabulary.

Ethics and Professionalism in Veterinary Practice

Ethics and professionalism form the cornerstone of veterinary practice, guiding veterinarians in their interactions with animals, clients, and colleagues. They are the compass that navigates the complex landscape of animal care, where decisions often impact not only the health and well-being of creatures but also the trust and expectations of their human caretakers. For those entering the field, understanding and embodying these principles is essential for building a career characterized by integrity, respect, and compassion.

At its core, veterinary ethics is about making choices that prioritize the welfare of animals while balancing the needs and desires of clients. This often involves navigating difficult decisions, such as when to recommend euthanasia, how to manage limited resources, or how to handle cases of animal neglect or abuse. Each situation presents unique challenges, requiring veterinarians to weigh their professional responsibilities against personal values and societal expectations. The ability to make ethically sound decisions hinges on a deep understanding of ethical principles and the courage to act in the best interest of the patient, even in the face of adversity.

One foundational concept in veterinary ethics is the principle of "do no harm," which underscores the responsibility to avoid causing unnecessary suffering to animals. This principle is not always as straightforward as it seems, particularly in cases where treatment options might prolong suffering or when financial constraints limit access to care. Veterinarians must exercise sound judgment and empathy, considering the quality of life and long-term outcomes for the animals under their care. Open and honest communication with clients is crucial, ensuring that they have a clear understanding of the options and implications of different courses of action.

Confidentiality is another critical aspect of professionalism in veterinary practice. Just as in human medicine, veterinarians must respect the privacy of their clients and patients, safeguarding sensitive information shared during consultations. This includes medical records, personal information, and any observations made during visits. Maintaining confidentiality fosters trust and builds strong relationships with clients, which are essential for effective collaboration and care.

Professionalism also encompasses the duty to continually update one's knowledge and skills. The field of veterinary medicine is ever-evolving, with new research, technologies, and treatments emerging regularly. Veterinarians must commit to lifelong learning, participating in continuing education and staying informed about advancements in their areas of practice. This dedication to professional growth ensures that veterinarians can provide the highest standard of care and make informed decisions based on the latest evidence.

In the realm of client interactions, professionalism is demonstrated through effective communication, empathy, and respect. Veterinarians must be skilled at explaining complex medical information in a way that is understandable and accessible to clients, empowering them to make informed decisions about their pet's care. This involves active listening, addressing concerns, and providing reassurance, especially in emotionally charged situations. By fostering open dialogue and building rapport, veterinarians can create a supportive environment where clients feel valued and respected.

Ethical dilemmas often arise in the context of financial constraints, where clients may be unable to afford recommended treatments. Navigating these situations requires sensitivity and creativity, as veterinarians must balance the desire to provide optimal care with the reality of limited resources. Exploring alternative treatment options, discussing payment plans, or connecting clients with charitable organizations that offer financial assistance can help bridge the gap between ideal care and practical limitations. Transparency and honesty about costs and potential outcomes are essential, ensuring that clients have realistic expectations and can make decisions that align with their values and circumstances.

The ethical treatment of colleagues and staff is another important facet of professionalism. The veterinary workplace should be one of collaboration, respect, and mutual support, where all team members are valued for their contributions. This includes recognizing the diverse skills and expertise that each person brings, fostering an inclusive environment, and addressing conflicts constructively. By promoting a culture of professionalism and respect, veterinarians can create a positive and productive work environment that benefits both employees and clients.

Veterinarians also have a responsibility to advocate for animal welfare at a broader societal level. This may involve participating in public education campaigns, engaging with policy-making processes, or collaborating with animal welfare organizations. By using their expertise to influence positive change, veterinarians can contribute to the advancement of animal welfare standards and promote a more compassionate society.

Reflecting on one's own ethical beliefs and biases is a crucial component of ethical practice. Veterinarians must be aware of how their personal values and experiences may influence their professional decisions and interactions. Engaging in self-reflection and seeking diverse perspectives can help practitioners navigate ethical challenges with greater insight and objectivity. Additionally, participating in ethical discussions with peers and mentors can provide valuable guidance and support, enriching one's understanding of complex ethical issues.

Ethics and professionalism are not static concepts; they evolve alongside societal changes, scientific advancements, and shifting cultural norms. Veterinarians must remain adaptable and open-minded, willing to re-evaluate their practices and beliefs as new information and perspectives emerge. By embracing this dynamic approach, veterinarians can continue to provide ethically sound and professional care that meets the needs of the animals and communities they serve.

Chapter 3

Diagnostic Techniques and Tools

Physical Examination Basics

Conducting a comprehensive physical examination is a foundational skill in veterinary medicine, serving as the primary tool for assessing the health of animals. It is a methodical process that involves observing, palpating, and listening, enabling veterinarians to gather critical information about their patients. For those new to the practice, mastering the basics of physical examination is essential for building confidence and competence in clinical settings.

Approaching a physical examination requires a blend of technical skill and interpersonal finesse. Establishing a calm and trusting environment is the first step, as it sets the stage for a successful examination. Animals are highly perceptive, and their behavior can be influenced by the demeanor of the veterinarian. Approaching with a gentle and reassuring manner helps to alleviate anxiety, making the animal more receptive to handling. Taking a moment to observe the animal's behavior and demeanor before initiating the examination provides valuable context for assessing its overall condition.

The examination typically begins with a general assessment of the animal's appearance and behavior. Observing the animal from a distance allows for the evaluation of posture, gait, and any obvious abnormalities. This initial observation can reveal signs of pain, lameness, or neurological issues. Additionally, assessing the animal's demeanor—whether it appears alert, lethargic, anxious, or aggressive—provides insights into its mental and physical state.

Moving closer, a systematic approach is essential to ensure a thorough examination. Starting at the head and progressing towards the tail helps maintain consistency and ensures that no areas are overlooked. The head examination involves assessing the eyes, ears, nose, and mouth. Checking the eyes for clarity, discharge, or redness can indicate underlying health issues such as infections or allergies. Examining the ears for signs of wax buildup, odor, or inflammation helps identify potential ear infections or infestations. Inspecting the nose for discharge or crusting can provide clues about respiratory health, while examining the mouth and teeth offers insights into dental hygiene and potential oral diseases.

Palpation of the neck and lymph nodes follows, checking for any swelling or abnormalities. Enlarged lymph nodes may be indicative of infection or systemic disease, necessitating further investigation. The neck is also palpated for any signs of pain or discomfort, which could suggest musculoskeletal or neurological issues.

Continuing to the thorax, auscultation of the heart and lungs is performed using a stethoscope. This involves listening to the heart for rate, rhythm, and any abnormal sounds such as murmurs. Evaluating the lung fields for clear, equal breath sounds is crucial for identifying respiratory issues like pneumonia or asthma. Auscultation requires practice and patience, as distinguishing subtle nuances in sounds is a skill developed over time.

The abdomen is palpated to assess the size, shape, and consistency of internal organs. This part of the examination can reveal abnormalities such as masses, fluid accumulation, or organ enlargement. Gentle and systematic palpation helps avoid discomfort and ensures the accurate detection of abnormalities. Observing the animal's reaction to palpation is also important, as signs of pain or discomfort can indicate underlying issues.

Examining the musculoskeletal system involves assessing the limbs, joints, and spine for signs of swelling, pain, or limited range of motion. Evaluating the gait and posture provides additional information about musculoskeletal health, aiding in the diagnosis of injuries or degenerative conditions. Gently manipulating each limb and joint helps identify areas of concern, allowing for targeted diagnostics and treatment.

The integumentary system, including the skin, coat, and nails, is assessed for signs of dermatological issues. Inspecting the skin for lesions, parasites, or signs of infection is essential, as dermatological conditions are common in veterinary practice. The coat's texture and condition offer insights into the animal's overall health and nutrition, while the nails are checked for appropriate length and any signs of trauma or disease.

The final component of the physical examination involves assessing the animal's body condition score

(BCS) and weight. The BCS is a subjective measure of an animal's fat stores, providing a useful indicator of nutritional status. It ranges from emaciated to obese, with a healthy BCS falling in the middle of the scale. Monitoring weight and BCS over time helps track an animal's health and identify potential issues related to diet or metabolism.

Throughout the examination, clear and concise documentation is essential. Recording findings, measurements, and observations ensures that all relevant information is captured and can be referenced in the future. Accurate documentation also facilitates communication with other veterinary professionals and supports continuity of care.

A successful physical examination is not solely about identifying abnormalities; it is also an opportunity to establish rapport with clients and educate them about their pet's health. Communicating findings and recommendations in an empathetic and understandable manner empowers clients to make informed decisions about their animal's care. Providing guidance on preventive measures, such as vaccinations, parasite control, and nutrition, further enhances the value of the examination.

Laboratory Diagnostics Blood, Urine, and Tissue Testing

Laboratory diagnostics are a cornerstone of veterinary medicine, providing invaluable insights into the health and well-being of animals. Blood, urine, and tissue testing are among the most common diagnostic tools employed by veterinarians, each offering a unique window into the physiological state of a patient. These tests help detect diseases, monitor health conditions, and guide treatment decisions, making them essential components of comprehensive veterinary care.

Blood testing, also known as hematology, involves analyzing the components and properties of blood to assess an animal's overall health. A complete blood count (CBC) is one of the most frequently performed blood tests, providing detailed information about red blood cells, white blood cells, and platelets. The CBC can reveal a wealth of information, such as anemia, infection, inflammation, and clotting disorders. For instance, a high white blood cell count might indicate an infection or inflammatory process, while low red blood cell levels could suggest anemia or blood loss.

In addition to the CBC, blood chemistry panels measure various enzymes, electrolytes, and metabolites in the blood. These tests provide insights into the function of organs such as the liver, kidneys, and pancreas. Elevated liver enzymes, for instance, may signal liver disease or damage, while abnormal electrolyte levels can indicate imbalances affecting the heart, muscles, or nervous system. Blood chemistry panels are valuable tools for detecting systemic diseases and monitoring the effectiveness of ongoing treatments.

Urine testing, or urinalysis, complements blood tests by providing information about kidney function, hydration status, and metabolic processes. A urinalysis evaluates several parameters, including color, clarity, pH, and the presence of substances like glucose, protein, and blood. The presence of glucose in urine, for example, can be indicative of diabetes mellitus, while proteinuria may suggest kidney dysfunction or disease. Microscopic examination of urine sediment can also reveal crystals, bacteria, or cells that provide further clues about underlying health issues.

Tissue testing, often conducted through biopsy or cytology, involves the examination of cells or tissue samples to diagnose diseases or assess the severity of a condition. Biopsy involves the removal of a small tissue sample for histopathological examination under a microscope. This technique is particularly useful for diagnosing tumors, inflammatory conditions, and autoimmune diseases. A biopsy can confirm malignancy in a suspected cancerous mass or determine the cause of chronic inflammation in an organ.

Cytology, on the other hand, involves the study of individual cells, often obtained through fine-needle aspiration or swabbing. It is a less invasive method than biopsy and is commonly used to evaluate skin lesions, lymph nodes, and masses. Cytology can provide rapid insights into infections, inflammation, and cancer, helping veterinarians make informed decisions about further diagnostic testing or treatment options.

The interpretation of laboratory results requires a comprehensive understanding of normal reference ranges and the ability to recognize patterns indicative of specific diseases or conditions. It is important for veterinarians to consider the entire clinical picture, integrating laboratory findings with physical examination results and the animal's medical history. This holistic approach aids in formulating accurate diagnoses and developing effective treatment plans.

Quality control and assurance are critical aspects of laboratory diagnostics, ensuring that test results are accurate and reliable. Veterinary professionals must adhere to standardized protocols for sample collection, handling, and analysis to minimize the risk of errors or contamination. Proper labeling, storage, and timely processing of samples are essential for maintaining the integrity of test results. Additionally, veterinarians should collaborate with reputable laboratories that employ rigorous quality control measures and provide expert interpretation of complex results.

Effective communication with pet owners about laboratory diagnostics is essential for fostering understanding and trust in the veterinary process. Veterinarians should explain the purpose and significance of each test, what the results may indicate, and how they will inform the animal's care plan. Providing clear and concise information empowers pet owners to make informed decisions and actively participate in their pet's health management.

In some cases, advanced diagnostic techniques such as imaging or specialized blood tests may be necessary to further investigate complex conditions. Techniques like ultrasound, radiography, and MRI provide detailed visual information about internal structures, while tests like hormone assays or genetic screening offer insights into specific diseases. Veterinarians should be prepared to discuss these options with pet

owners, explaining the benefits, limitations, and
potential outcomes of additional testing.

The role of laboratory diagnostics extends beyond
individual patient care, contributing to the broader
understanding of animal health and disease. Data
collected from routine tests can be used for
epidemiological studies, tracking disease trends, and
developing preventive health strategies. By
participating in research and data sharing initiatives,
veterinarians can contribute to the advancement of
veterinary medicine and the improvement of animal
welfare on a larger scale.

Staying abreast of advancements in laboratory
diagnostics is crucial for veterinarians, as new
technologies and techniques continue to emerge.
Innovations such as point-of-care testing, molecular
diagnostics, and personalized medicine are reshaping
the landscape of veterinary diagnostics, offering new
possibilities for early detection and targeted treatment
of diseases. Engaging in continuing education and
collaborating with experts in the field help
veterinarians stay informed about these developments
and incorporate them into their practice.

Imaging Techniques X-Rays, Ultrasounds, and MRIs

In the realm of veterinary diagnostics, imaging
techniques such as X-rays, ultrasounds, and MRIs
play a pivotal role in unveiling the internal landscapes
of animal bodies. These non-invasive methods allow
veterinarians to visualize organs, tissues, and skeletal

structures, providing crucial insights that guide diagnosis and treatment. For those new to the field, understanding the principles and applications of these imaging techniques is essential for delivering comprehensive veterinary care.

X-rays, or radiographs, are among the most commonly used imaging tools in veterinary practice. They operate on the principle of differential absorption, where X-ray beams pass through the body and are absorbed at varying degrees by different tissues. Bones, being dense, absorb more X-rays and appear white on the radiograph, while softer tissues like muscles and organs appear in shades of gray. X-rays are particularly useful for diagnosing fractures, detecting foreign objects, and evaluating the condition of joints and bones. In cases of respiratory distress, chest radiographs can reveal abnormalities such as pneumonia, tumors, or fluid accumulation.

Despite their widespread use, X-rays have limitations. They provide two-dimensional images, which can make it challenging to discern complex structures or overlapping tissues. Additionally, the exposure to ionizing radiation, although minimal, necessitates the use of protective measures for both staff and patients. Proper positioning and restraint are crucial for obtaining clear and diagnostic images, requiring skill and patience, especially when dealing with anxious or uncooperative animals.

Ultrasound imaging, or sonography, complements X-rays by providing real-time, three-dimensional images of soft tissues. It utilizes high-frequency sound waves that bounce off internal structures, creating echoes that are transformed into visual images. Ultrasound is highly effective for examining the abdomen, heart, and reproductive organs. It is invaluable in diagnosing conditions such as pregnancy, tumors, cysts, and fluid accumulations. One of the key advantages of ultrasound is its ability to visualize movement, allowing veterinarians to assess blood flow and organ function dynamically.

The non-invasive nature of ultrasound, coupled with the absence of radiation, makes it a safe and versatile tool for repeated examinations. It does, however, require considerable expertise to interpret the images accurately. The quality of the ultrasound image depends on factors such as the frequency of the sound waves, the skill of the operator, and the animal's body condition. Veterinarians must be adept at adjusting settings and positioning the transducer to capture the best possible images.

Magnetic Resonance Imaging (MRI) represents the pinnacle of veterinary imaging, offering unparalleled detail and contrast for soft tissue evaluation. MRI uses powerful magnets and radio waves to generate detailed cross-sectional images of the body. It is particularly useful for examining the brain, spinal cord, and joints, providing insights into neurological disorders, intervertebral disc disease, and complex musculoskeletal conditions. The ability to differentiate between various tissue types with high precision makes MRI an invaluable tool for diagnosing conditions that are difficult to assess with other imaging modalities.

However, the sophistication of MRI comes with certain challenges. The procedure requires general anesthesia to prevent movement, as even slight motion can render images unusable. The cost and availability of MRI are also considerations, as it is typically more expensive and less accessible than X-rays or ultrasound. Despite these challenges, MRI remains an essential diagnostic tool, especially for complex cases where other imaging techniques fall short.

The selection of an appropriate imaging technique depends on several factors, including the clinical question, the area of interest, and the animal's condition. Often, a combination of imaging modalities is employed to provide a comprehensive assessment. For example, X-rays may be used to identify a fracture, while ultrasound can assess soft tissue damage surrounding the injury. In cases of suspected neurological disorders, MRI might be the preferred choice for its ability to provide detailed images of the nervous system.

Effective communication with pet owners is crucial when discussing imaging options. Veterinarians should explain the purpose, benefits, and limitations of each technique, as well as any potential risks or costs involved. Providing clear information empowers owners to make informed decisions about their pet's care and fosters trust in the veterinary process.

As technology continues to advance, the capabilities of imaging techniques are expanding, offering new possibilities for diagnosis and treatment. Innovations such as digital radiography, 3D ultrasound, and advanced MRI sequences are enhancing the accuracy and efficiency of veterinary imaging. Staying informed about these developments and incorporating them into practice ensures that veterinarians can offer the best possible care to their patients.

Training and experience play a significant role in the successful use of imaging techniques. Veterinarians and technicians must develop a keen eye for detail and a strong understanding of anatomy to interpret images accurately. Continuing education and collaboration with specialists can enhance proficiency and confidence in using these diagnostic tools.

Advances in Diagnostic Technology

The landscape of veterinary medicine has been transformed by advances in diagnostic technology, revolutionizing the way veterinarians approach animal health care. As cutting-edge tools and techniques become increasingly integrated into practice, they offer unprecedented opportunities for accurate diagnosis, early detection, and personalized treatment plans. For those embarking on a veterinary career, understanding these technological advancements is crucial for staying at the forefront of the profession.

One of the most significant breakthroughs in diagnostic technology is the advent of digital radiography. Unlike traditional X-ray film, digital radiography captures images electronically, allowing for immediate viewing and manipulation. This technology provides several advantages, including enhanced image quality, reduced radiation exposure, and the ability to easily share images with specialists for consultation. The immediacy of digital radiography enables veterinarians to make quicker, more informed decisions, improving patient outcomes and streamlining workflows.

Another remarkable advancement is the development of point-of-care testing (POCT) devices, which allow for rapid diagnostic testing directly in the veterinary clinic. These portable devices can perform a wide range of tests, from blood chemistry panels to infectious disease screenings, providing results within minutes. POCT is particularly valuable in emergency and critical care settings, where timely information can be life-saving. By facilitating immediate decision-making, these devices enhance the efficiency of veterinary practice and improve the standard of care.

The field of molecular diagnostics has also seen significant progress, with techniques such as polymerase chain reaction (PCR) and next-generation sequencing (NGS) becoming more accessible and affordable. PCR allows for the detection of specific genetic material, making it a powerful tool for identifying infectious agents and genetic disorders. NGS, on the other hand, enables comprehensive analysis of entire genomes, offering insights into complex diseases and genetic predispositions. These molecular techniques have expanded the diagnostic capabilities of veterinarians, providing precise and reliable answers to challenging clinical questions.

In the realm of imaging, advancements such as computed tomography (CT) and three-dimensional (3D) imaging have elevated the standard of diagnostic care. CT scans provide detailed cross-sectional images of the body, offering unparalleled insights into complex anatomical structures. This technology is invaluable for diagnosing conditions such as tumors, fractures, and vascular anomalies. The ability to create 3D reconstructions of CT data further enhances visualization, aiding in surgical planning and treatment monitoring.

Ultrasound technology has also evolved, with the introduction of high-resolution and Doppler ultrasound systems. These advancements allow for more detailed examination of soft tissues, blood flow, and organ function. High-resolution ultrasound provides clearer images, facilitating the detection of subtle abnormalities, while Doppler ultrasound measures blood flow velocity, aiding in the assessment of cardiovascular health. These innovations have expanded the diagnostic capabilities of ultrasound, making it an indispensable tool in veterinary practice.

Telemedicine is another area where diagnostic technology is making a significant impact. By leveraging digital communication platforms, veterinarians can consult with specialists, review diagnostic images, and provide remote care to patients. Telemedicine expands access to veterinary expertise, particularly in rural or underserved areas, and enhances collaboration among veterinary professionals. As technology continues to advance, the scope of telemedicine is likely to grow, offering new possibilities for veterinary care delivery.

Artificial intelligence (AI) and machine learning are emerging technologies with the potential to transform diagnostic processes. AI algorithms can analyze large datasets, identify patterns, and generate insights that may be challenging for humans to discern. In veterinary diagnostics, AI has been applied to image analysis, disease prediction, and personalized treatment recommendations. While still in its early stages, the integration of AI into veterinary practice holds promise for enhancing diagnostic accuracy and improving patient care.

The rise of wearable technology and remote monitoring devices is also shaping the future of veterinary diagnostics. These devices, which can be worn by animals, collect real-time data on vital signs, activity levels, and environmental conditions. By providing continuous monitoring, they enable early detection of health issues and facilitate proactive management of chronic conditions. The data collected can be integrated into electronic health records, offering a comprehensive view of an animal's health status and informing personalized care plans.

As diagnostic technology continues to evolve, veterinarians must stay informed and adapt to new tools and techniques. Continuing education and professional development are essential for maintaining proficiency and ensuring the best possible care for patients. Embracing these advancements not only enhances diagnostic capabilities but also empowers veterinarians to provide more effective, efficient, and compassionate care.

The integration of advanced diagnostic technology into veterinary practice also presents ethical considerations. Veterinarians must balance the benefits of new technologies with considerations of cost, accessibility, and the welfare of their patients.

Informed consent and clear communication with pet owners are crucial, ensuring that they understand the purpose, benefits, and potential risks of diagnostic procedures. By navigating these challenges with integrity and transparency, veterinarians can uphold the highest standards of ethical practice.

The future of veterinary diagnostics is bright, with ongoing innovations poised to further transform the field. From personalized medicine to predictive analytics, the possibilities are vast, offering new avenues for improving animal health and welfare. As technology continues to advance, veterinarians are uniquely positioned to harness these tools, shaping the future of veterinary medicine and enhancing the lives of animals and their human companions.

Interpreting Diagnostic Results

Interpreting diagnostic results is a critical skill in veterinary practice, one that bridges the gap between raw data and informed clinical decision-making. The ability to accurately interpret results from various diagnostic tests not only aids in identifying the underlying causes of an animal's condition but also guides the formulation of effective treatment plans. This chapter delves into the nuances of interpreting diagnostic results, offering practical insights and strategies for beginners to navigate this complex task.

The first step in interpreting diagnostic results is understanding the reference ranges for each test. Reference ranges represent the expected values for a healthy population of a particular species, taking into account factors such as age, sex, and breed. These ranges provide a baseline for comparison, allowing veterinarians to identify deviations that may indicate underlying health issues. However, it's essential to remember that reference ranges are guidelines, not absolutes. Individual variations exist, and results must be interpreted in the context of the animal's overall health, clinical signs, and medical history.

Consider, for example, a dog presenting with lethargy and decreased appetite. Blood tests reveal elevated liver enzymes, which fall outside the normal reference range. While this finding suggests liver dysfunction, it doesn't pinpoint the exact cause. The elevation could result from various conditions, such as hepatic lipidosis, infectious hepatitis, or exposure to toxins. Here, the veterinarian must integrate the laboratory results with clinical observations, the dog's history, and any additional diagnostics performed, such as imaging or biopsy, to arrive at a conclusive diagnosis.

Pattern recognition plays a crucial role in interpreting diagnostic results. Certain combinations of abnormalities can suggest specific disease processes. For instance, a complete blood count (CBC) showing anemia, leukocytosis, and thrombocytopenia may indicate an inflammatory or infectious process. By recognizing these patterns, veterinarians can narrow down potential differential diagnoses and focus on further testing or treatments that address the underlying cause.

It's also vital to consider the sensitivity and specificity of diagnostic tests. Sensitivity refers to a test's ability to correctly identify those with the disease (true positives), while specificity relates to its ability to correctly identify those without the disease (true negatives). A highly sensitive test is useful for ruling out a disease, as a negative result is likely to be accurate. Conversely, a highly specific test is valuable for confirming a disease, as a positive result is more reliable. Balancing sensitivity and specificity is key to choosing the right test and interpreting its results accurately.

False positives and false negatives are inherent risks in diagnostic testing. A false positive occurs when a test indicates the presence of a disease that isn't actually there, leading to unnecessary stress and possibly unneeded treatments. On the other hand, a false negative indicates that a disease is absent when it is present, potentially delaying critical intervention. Understanding the limitations of each test and the potential for these errors helps veterinarians make more informed decisions.

Communication with pet owners is a crucial aspect of interpreting diagnostic results. It's important to explain the findings clearly and concisely, avoiding overly technical language that may confuse or overwhelm. Veterinarians should discuss the implications of the results, potential diagnoses, and the next steps in the diagnostic or treatment process. This dialogue fosters trust and collaboration, ensuring that pet owners are actively involved in their animal's care.

Interpreting diagnostic results isn't solely about identifying disease; it's also about monitoring health and treatment progress. Regular testing, such as blood work or urinalysis, can track the effectiveness of treatments and provide early warning signs of potential issues. For animals with chronic conditions, periodic assessments help adjust management plans to maintain optimal health and quality of life.

Experience and continuous learning are fundamental to mastering the interpretation of diagnostic results. Veterinary professionals should engage in ongoing education, attend workshops, and collaborate with colleagues to stay current with advancements in diagnostic techniques and interpretation. Peer-reviewed journals and case studies can offer valuable insights into the complexities of diagnostic interpretation and the nuances of specific cases.

The role of intuition should not be underestimated in the interpretation process. While data and reference ranges provide a foundation, a veterinarian's intuition, honed through experience and observation, can offer unique insights into a case. This intuitive understanding often guides further testing or investigation, leading to more accurate diagnoses and better patient outcomes.

Ethical considerations also come into play when interpreting diagnostic results. Veterinarians must weigh the benefits and risks of further testing or treatments, considering the animal's welfare, the owner's resources, and the potential outcomes. Transparent and compassionate communication is essential, ensuring that decisions are made in the best interest of the animal and with the owner's informed consent.

In the ever-evolving field of veterinary medicine, technological advancements continue to enhance diagnostic capabilities, offering more detailed and comprehensive results. However, the core principles of interpretation remain grounded in a holistic approach—integrating results with clinical observations, history, and experience to provide the best possible care for animal patients.

Chapter 4
Medical Treatments and Procedures

Pharmacology Essentials for Veterinarians

Pharmacology forms the backbone of veterinary therapeutics, equipping veterinarians with the knowledge and tools necessary to treat a wide range of animal ailments. Understanding the principles of pharmacology is essential for ensuring the safe and effective use of medications in veterinary practice. This chapter provides an overview of pharmacology essentials, offering practical guidance for those new to the field.

At its core, pharmacology is the study of how drugs interact with biological systems. It encompasses the understanding of drug properties, mechanisms of action, therapeutic uses, and potential side effects. For veterinarians, this knowledge is crucial in selecting appropriate medications, determining dosages, and anticipating possible adverse reactions.

One of the key concepts in pharmacology is the mechanism of action, which describes how a drug produces its effects in the body. This can involve interactions with receptors, enzymes, ion channels, or other cellular targets. For example, nonsteroidal anti-inflammatory drugs (NSAIDs) alleviate pain and inflammation by inhibiting the cyclooxygenase (COX) enzymes, which play a role in prostaglandin synthesis.

Understanding a drug's mechanism of action helps veterinarians predict its therapeutic effects and potential side effects.

Dosage determination is another critical aspect of pharmacology. Accurate dosing ensures that a drug achieves its desired effect without causing harm. Dosage calculations typically consider the animal's weight, age, species, and health status. In some cases, therapeutic drug monitoring may be necessary to adjust doses based on individual responses. For instance, the dosage of certain anticonvulsants may need adjustment based on blood levels to achieve optimal seizure control.

Pharmacokinetics and pharmacodynamics are intertwined concepts that influence drug action. Pharmacokinetics describes the absorption, distribution, metabolism, and excretion of drugs, collectively known as ADME. These processes determine the concentration of a drug at its site of action and influence the onset, duration, and intensity of its effects. For instance, a drug with rapid absorption and slow elimination may be administered less frequently than one with slow absorption and rapid elimination.

Pharmacodynamics, on the other hand, focuses on the relationship between drug concentration and its effects on the body. It helps veterinarians understand the dose-response relationship and identify the therapeutic window—the range of drug concentrations that produce the desired effects without causing toxicity. A narrow therapeutic window requires precise dosing and careful monitoring to avoid adverse effects.

Species-specific considerations are paramount in veterinary pharmacology, as animals can exhibit significant differences in drug metabolism and response. For example, cats lack certain liver enzymes, making them more susceptible to toxicity from drugs like acetaminophen. Horses, with their unique gastrointestinal physiology, may absorb oral medications differently than small animals. Understanding these species-specific differences is crucial for avoiding adverse reactions and optimizing treatment outcomes.

Adverse drug reactions (ADRs) are an inherent risk of pharmacotherapy and can range from mild to life-threatening. Recognizing and managing ADRs is a vital skill for veterinarians. Common reactions include gastrointestinal upset, allergic reactions, and organ toxicity. In some cases, drug interactions can exacerbate ADRs, highlighting the importance of a thorough medication history before prescribing new treatments. Educating pet owners about potential side effects and monitoring for signs of ADRs ensures prompt intervention when necessary.

Veterinarians must also consider legal and ethical aspects of drug use, including regulations governing the prescription and dispensing of medications. Familiarity with the laws surrounding controlled substances, off-label use, and compounding is essential for maintaining compliance and safeguarding animal welfare. Informed consent is a critical component, requiring veterinarians to discuss the risks, benefits, and alternatives of treatments with pet owners.

Antimicrobial stewardship is an increasingly important aspect of veterinary pharmacology, addressing the global challenge of antimicrobial resistance. Responsible use of antibiotics involves selecting appropriate agents based on culture and sensitivity testing, using the narrowest spectrum effective, and adhering to recommended dosages and treatment durations. Educating pet owners about the importance of completing antibiotic courses and preventing the misuse of leftover medications is vital for preserving the efficacy of these critical drugs.

The role of pharmacology extends beyond treatment to include preventive care and disease management. Vaccinations, an essential component of preventive medicine, rely on pharmacological principles to stimulate immune responses and protect against infectious diseases. Parasiticides, used to control internal and external parasites, play a crucial role in maintaining animal health and preventing zoonotic transmission. Understanding the pharmacology of these agents ensures their safe and effective use in diverse settings.

Continuing education and staying informed about new developments in pharmacology are essential for veterinary professionals. Advances in drug formulations, novel therapeutic agents, and emerging resistance patterns require veterinarians to remain up-to-date with the latest research and guidelines. Collaboration with pharmacists and specialists can enhance understanding and improve patient outcomes.

Effective communication is key to successful pharmacotherapy. Veterinarians must convey clear instructions to pet owners regarding medication administration, storage, and monitoring. Demonstrating proper techniques, such as pill administration or topical application, can improve compliance and treatment success. Addressing questions and concerns with empathy and expertise fosters trust and ensures that pet owners are active participants in their animal's care.

Common Medical Conditions and Treatments

Veterinary medicine is a vast field that encompasses a myriad of medical conditions affecting various species. For newcomers to the field, gaining a solid understanding of common medical conditions and their treatments is essential. This knowledge not only enhances diagnostic acumen but also informs the development of effective treatment plans tailored to each animal's unique needs.

One prevalent condition that veterinarians often encounter is osteoarthritis, particularly in older dogs and cats. This degenerative joint disease is characterized by the breakdown of cartilage, leading to pain and decreased mobility. Treatment strategies typically include a combination of weight management, exercise modification, and pharmacologic interventions such as nonsteroidal anti-inflammatory drugs (NSAIDs). In some cases, nutritional supplements like glucosamine and chondroitin sulfate may be recommended to support joint health. Physical therapy and alternative treatments, such as acupuncture, can further aid in alleviating discomfort and improving quality of life.

Gastrointestinal disorders are another common issue in veterinary practice, affecting pets of all ages. Vomiting and diarrhea can result from a variety of causes, including dietary indiscretion, infections, or underlying systemic diseases. Initial treatment often involves dietary modification, such as introducing a bland diet, and ensuring adequate hydration. In cases of bacterial or parasitic infections, appropriate antimicrobial or antiparasitic medications are prescribed. Chronic gastrointestinal conditions, such as inflammatory bowel disease (IBD), require more complex management, often involving long-term dietary changes and immune-modulating drugs.

Dermatological conditions, including allergies and infections, frequently present in veterinary clinics. Allergies in pets can manifest as itchy skin, ear infections, and gastrointestinal upset. Identifying and eliminating the allergen, whether it be food-related or environmental, is key to managing these conditions. Antihistamines, corticosteroids, and immune-modulating drugs are commonly used to alleviate symptoms. For bacterial or fungal skin infections, topical or systemic antimicrobials are indicated. Regular grooming and appropriate skin care can also help prevent and manage dermatological issues.

Infectious diseases pose significant challenges in veterinary medicine, with prevention and early detection being crucial. Canine parvovirus, for example, is a highly contagious viral disease that causes severe gastrointestinal symptoms and can be fatal if untreated. Vaccination remains the most effective preventive measure. Infected dogs require intensive supportive care, including fluid therapy and nutritional support. Similarly, feline upper respiratory infections, commonly caused by viruses such as herpesvirus and calicivirus, are managed through supportive care, antiviral medications, and environmental management to reduce stress.

Endocrine disorders, such as diabetes mellitus and hyperthyroidism, are prevalent in both dogs and cats. Diabetes is characterized by an inability to regulate blood sugar levels, often necessitating insulin therapy and dietary management. Blood glucose monitoring and regular veterinary check-ups are essential for managing this condition effectively. Hyperthyroidism, commonly seen in older cats, results from excessive thyroid hormone production, leading to weight loss, increased appetite, and hyperactivity. Treatment options include medication, dietary management, or more definitive interventions like radioactive iodine therapy or surgery.

Cardiovascular conditions, such as heart disease, are also commonly diagnosed in veterinary practice. Mitral valve disease, prevalent in small breed dogs, leads to heart murmurs, coughing, and exercise intolerance. Management focuses on controlling symptoms and improving quality of life through medications that reduce fluid accumulation and support heart function. In cats, hypertrophic cardiomyopathy is a common cardiac condition characterized by thickening of the heart muscle. Treatment involves medications to manage heart rate and reduce the risk of blood clots, along with regular monitoring to assess disease progression.

Renal disease, particularly chronic kidney disease, is frequently seen in older cats and dogs. It results from the gradual loss of kidney function, leading to the accumulation of waste products in the blood. Management strategies include dietary modification to reduce protein and phosphorus intake, ensuring adequate hydration, and addressing any concurrent conditions, such as hypertension. Regular monitoring of kidney function and adjustments to treatment plans are necessary to slow disease progression and maintain quality of life.

Neurological disorders, such as epilepsy, require careful management and monitoring. Epileptic seizures can vary in frequency and severity, necessitating a tailored approach to treatment. Antiepileptic medications, such as phenobarbital or levetiracetam, are commonly used to control seizures. Regular blood tests and veterinary consultations help ensure the effectiveness of treatment and minimize side effects. In addition to medication, identifying and avoiding potential triggers can help reduce the frequency of seizures.

Cancer is a significant concern in veterinary medicine, with advancements in diagnosis and treatment improving outcomes for affected animals. Treatment options include surgery, chemotherapy, radiation therapy, and palliative care, depending on the type and stage of cancer. A multidisciplinary approach, often involving specialists, is essential for developing a comprehensive treatment plan that considers the animal's overall health, quality of life, and the owner's preferences.

Preventive care plays a vital role in managing common medical conditions and promoting overall health. Regular veterinary check-ups, vaccinations, parasite control, and dental care are essential components of preventive health care. Educating pet owners about the importance of these measures empowers them to take an active role in their pet's well-being and helps detect potential health issues early, when they are most manageable.

Effective communication with pet owners is crucial in managing common medical conditions. Veterinarians must provide clear explanations of diagnoses, treatment options, and potential outcomes. Addressing concerns and answering questions with empathy fosters trust and collaboration, ensuring that pet owners feel supported and involved in their pet's care.

Emergency Care and First Aid

Emergencies in veterinary medicine often occur without warning, thrusting both pet owners and veterinarians into situations that demand quick thinking and decisive action. Understanding the fundamentals of emergency care and first aid is crucial for anyone involved in animal care, from new veterinary professionals to pet owners. This chapter outlines essential steps and considerations in handling animal emergencies, ensuring that each patient receives timely and effective care.

When an emergency strikes, the first step is to remain calm and assess the situation. Panic can cloud judgment and hinder the ability to make sound decisions, whereas a composed demeanor allows for clear thinking and effective response. Observing the animal's overall condition is crucial in determining the severity of the emergency. Key indicators include the animal's level of consciousness, breathing patterns, heart rate, and the presence of any visible injuries or bleeding. This initial assessment provides vital information for prioritizing actions and deciding the next steps.

One of the most common emergencies encountered in veterinary practice is trauma, which can result from accidents, falls, or animal attacks. In such cases, controlling bleeding is a top priority. Applying direct pressure with a clean cloth or bandage helps stem blood flow, while elevating the injured area, if possible, can reduce bleeding. In instances of severe hemorrhage, a tourniquet may be necessary, but it should be used with caution and only as a last resort.

Another critical aspect of emergency care is ensuring the animal's airway is clear and that they are breathing adequately. If the animal is unconscious and not breathing, administering cardiopulmonary resuscitation (CPR) may be necessary. CPR for animals involves chest compressions and rescue breaths, similar to the procedure for humans, but with modifications based on the animal's size and anatomy. Familiarity with species-specific CPR techniques is essential for veterinary professionals, as prompt intervention can be life-saving.

Shock is a life-threatening condition that can accompany various emergencies, including trauma, poisoning, and severe allergic reactions. Recognizing the signs of shock, such as pale gums, rapid heart rate, weak pulse, and rapid breathing, is crucial for prompt intervention. Maintaining the animal's body temperature, providing oxygen, and ensuring adequate blood flow are essential components of shock management. Immediate veterinary attention is vital, as untreated shock can lead to organ failure and death.

Poisoning is another emergency that requires swift action. Common household items, such as chocolate, antifreeze, and certain plants, can be toxic to animals. If poisoning is suspected, identifying the substance ingested and the amount consumed is crucial for guiding treatment. Inducing vomiting may be appropriate in some cases, but it is important to consult a veterinarian or poison control center for guidance. Administering activated charcoal can help absorb toxins in the gastrointestinal tract, while intravenous fluids and supportive care may be necessary to address systemic effects.

Heatstroke is a critical condition that can occur when animals are exposed to high temperatures and humidity, often due to being left in hot environments without adequate ventilation or water. Recognizing the signs of heatstroke, such as excessive panting, drooling, lethargy, and collapse, is vital for prompt intervention. Cooling the animal with lukewarm water, providing shade, and offering small amounts of water can help lower their body temperature. However, rapid cooling should be avoided, as it can lead to shock.

Seizures are another emergency that can be distressing for both the animal and the owner. Ensuring the animal's safety by removing nearby objects and preventing falls is essential. Seizures typically last a few minutes, and it's important not to restrain the animal during the episode. After the seizure subsides, keeping the animal calm and quiet is crucial. Veterinary evaluation is necessary to determine the underlying cause and prevent further episodes.

Injuries to the eyes or ears require careful handling to prevent further damage. If an eye injury is suspected, keeping the animal calm and avoiding pressure on the affected area is important. A clean, damp cloth can be used to gently wipe away any discharge, but further treatment should be left to a veterinarian. Ear injuries or foreign objects in the ear canal should also be addressed by a professional to avoid complications.

Burns and scalds, though less common, are emergencies that require immediate attention. Cooling the affected area with copious amounts of cool water can help reduce tissue damage. Covering the burn with a sterile dressing and avoiding the application of creams or ointments is recommended until veterinary care is available. Pain management and infection prevention are key components of burn treatment.

Fractures and dislocations can occur due to trauma or falls, necessitating careful handling to prevent exacerbating the injury. Immobilizing the affected limb with a splint or bandage can help prevent further damage during transport to the veterinary clinic. Pain management and radiographic evaluation are essential components of treatment, guiding decisions regarding surgical intervention or other therapies.

In the face of an emergency, communication with pet owners is critical. Providing clear instructions and reassurance can help alleviate anxiety and ensure that appropriate actions are taken. Educating pet owners about basic first aid techniques and the importance of seeking veterinary care for emergencies empowers them to act confidently and effectively in critical situations.

Preparation is key to effectively managing emergencies. Veterinary professionals should be well-versed in first aid techniques and have access to essential supplies, such as bandages, antiseptics, and emergency contact numbers. Regular training and drills can help maintain readiness and ensure that team members are prepared to respond swiftly and effectively when emergencies arise.

Pain Management and Anesthesia Techniques

In the realm of veterinary medicine, managing pain and administering anesthesia are integral components of providing compassionate and effective care for animal patients. Pain, whether acute or chronic, can significantly impact an animal's quality of life, influencing behavior, appetite, and overall well-being. Anesthesia, on the other hand, is essential for performing surgeries and diagnostic procedures safely and humanely. This chapter delves into the principles and practices of pain management and anesthesia, offering practical insights and guidance for those new to the field.

Understanding pain in animals begins with recognizing its manifestations, which can vary widely across species and individuals. Unlike humans, animals cannot verbally express their discomfort, making it crucial for veterinarians to rely on behavioral cues and physiological indicators. Changes in posture, vocalization, grooming habits, and appetite can signal pain, as can more subtle signs like restlessness or aggression. In some cases, physiological parameters such as heart rate, respiratory rate, and blood pressure may provide additional clues.

The cornerstone of effective pain management is a multimodal approach, which involves using a combination of therapies to address pain from multiple angles. This strategy maximizes efficacy while minimizing side effects, as lower doses of individual medications can be used. Nonsteroidal anti-inflammatory drugs (NSAIDs) are commonly employed to reduce inflammation and alleviate pain associated with conditions like arthritis or post-operative recovery. Opioids, such as morphine or buprenorphine, may be indicated for more severe pain, providing potent analgesic effects by acting on specific receptors in the nervous system.

Adjunctive therapies, including local anesthetics, can enhance pain management protocols by targeting specific areas. For instance, a local block may be administered during dental procedures to numb the surgical site, reducing the need for systemic analgesics. Other adjuncts, such as gabapentin or amantadine, can be used to manage neuropathic pain, which arises from nerve damage and may not respond well to traditional analgesics.

Non-pharmacological interventions also play a vital role in pain management. Physical therapy, acupuncture, and laser therapy are among the modalities that can support recovery and alleviate discomfort. These approaches not only address pain but also promote healing and improve mobility, contributing to a holistic treatment plan.

Anesthesia in veterinary practice requires a thorough understanding of pharmacology, physiology, and monitoring techniques to ensure the safety and well-being of animal patients. Pre-anesthetic assessment is a critical first step, involving a comprehensive evaluation of the animal's medical history, physical condition, and any pre-existing conditions that may influence anesthesia risk. This assessment guides the selection of anesthetic agents and protocols tailored to the individual patient.

The choice of anesthetic agents depends on several factors, including the type of procedure, the animal's species and size, and any concurrent medications. Injectable anesthetics, such as propofol or ketamine, offer rapid induction and recovery, making them suitable for short procedures or as part of a balanced anesthesia plan. Inhalant anesthetics, such as isoflurane or sevoflurane, provide precise control over anesthesia depth and are often used for longer surgeries.

Monitoring during anesthesia is essential for detecting and addressing potential complications. Parameters such as heart rate, respiratory rate, blood pressure, and oxygen saturation provide valuable information about the animal's physiological status. Capnography, which measures exhaled carbon dioxide, is another critical tool for assessing respiratory function. Regular monitoring ensures that any deviations from normal ranges are promptly identified and addressed, minimizing the risk of adverse events.

Recovery from anesthesia is a critical phase that requires careful observation and support. Ensuring a warm, quiet environment helps facilitate a smooth transition from anesthesia to consciousness. Monitoring vital signs and providing analgesics as needed are important components of post-operative care, ensuring that the animal remains comfortable and stable as they awaken and recover.

Effective communication with pet owners is an essential aspect of pain management and anesthesia. Educating owners about the procedures, potential risks, and expected outcomes fosters trust and collaboration. Providing clear instructions for post-operative care, such as medication administration and activity restrictions, ensures that owners can support their pet's recovery and identify any concerns that may arise.

Continuing education and staying abreast of advancements in pain management and anesthesia are crucial for veterinary professionals. New research and technologies continually enhance our understanding of analgesia and anesthetic techniques, offering opportunities to improve patient care and outcomes. Engaging in professional development, attending workshops, and collaborating with colleagues can help veterinarians refine their skills and expand their knowledge.

Ethical considerations are integral to pain management and anesthesia, underscoring the veterinarian's responsibility to prioritize the welfare and comfort of their patients. The judicious use of analgesics and anesthetics, combined with a commitment to minimizing pain and suffering, reflects the core values of veterinary medicine and the dedication to providing humane and compassionate care.

Holistic and Alternative Veterinary Medicine

Holistic and alternative veterinary medicine has gained traction in recent years as pet owners and veterinarians alike seek comprehensive approaches to animal health care. These practices emphasize treating the whole animal—mind, body, and spirit— rather than focusing solely on symptoms. This chapter delves into the principles, techniques, and benefits of holistic and alternative medicine in veterinary practice, offering insights into how these methods can complement traditional treatments.

Holistic veterinary medicine encompasses a variety of modalities, each aiming to support the animal's natural healing processes and enhance overall well- being. One foundational principle is the belief that the body has an innate ability to heal itself, given the right conditions. This approach often involves customizing treatment plans to address the unique needs of each animal, considering factors such as lifestyle, diet, environment, and emotional well-being.

Acupuncture, a well-known alternative therapy, has been practiced for thousands of years in traditional Chinese medicine. It involves inserting thin needles into specific points on the body to stimulate energy flow and promote balance. In veterinary medicine, acupuncture is often used to manage pain, support recovery from injury, and address chronic conditions such as arthritis and gastrointestinal disorders. Scientific studies have shown that acupuncture can stimulate the release of endorphins and other neurotransmitters, providing analgesic and anti-inflammatory effects.

Herbal medicine is another integral component of holistic veterinary care. Herbs have been used for centuries to treat various ailments and support health. In animals, herbal formulations may be used to boost the immune system, support liver function, or soothe anxious behavior. It's essential for veterinarians to have a thorough understanding of herbal pharmacology to avoid potential interactions with conventional medications and ensure safe and effective use. Consulting with a veterinary herbalist can provide valuable expertise in selecting appropriate herbs for specific conditions.

Homeopathy, based on the principle of "like cures like," involves using highly diluted substances to stimulate the body's self-healing mechanisms. While its efficacy is a subject of debate, some pet owners and veterinarians report positive outcomes using homeopathic remedies for conditions such as allergies, skin issues, and behavioral problems.

Homeopathy's individualized approach aligns with the holistic philosophy of treating the whole animal rather than isolated symptoms.

Chiropractic care, focusing on the musculoskeletal system, is used to address issues related to spinal alignment and mobility. Misalignments, or subluxations, can lead to pain and impaired function, affecting an animal's quality of life. Chiropractic adjustments aim to restore proper alignment, alleviate discomfort, and enhance nervous system function. Veterinarians trained in animal chiropractic techniques can provide these adjustments as part of a comprehensive treatment plan for conditions like lameness, back pain, and stiffness.

Nutrition plays a pivotal role in holistic veterinary medicine, recognizing that diet is a cornerstone of health. A balanced, species-appropriate diet provides the essential nutrients required for growth, repair, and maintenance of bodily functions. Holistic veterinarians may recommend whole-food diets, raw feeding, or customized nutrition plans based on the animal's specific health needs. Supplements, such as omega-3 fatty acids, probiotics, and antioxidants, can also support health and address deficiencies.

Massage therapy and physical rehabilitation are valuable techniques for promoting healing and enhancing mobility. Massage increases circulation, reduces muscle tension, and supports lymphatic drainage, contributing to recovery from injury or surgery. Physical rehabilitation, including exercises and modalities like hydrotherapy, helps improve strength, flexibility, and coordination. These techniques are particularly beneficial for animals recovering from orthopedic surgery or managing chronic conditions like arthritis.

The integration of holistic and alternative therapies with conventional veterinary medicine requires careful consideration and collaboration. Open communication between veterinarians and pet owners is essential to ensure that all aspects of the animal's care are aligned and complementary. Educating pet owners about the benefits and limitations of each modality empowers them to make informed decisions about their pet's health care.

It's important to recognize that holistic and alternative therapies should not replace conventional treatments in cases where medical intervention is necessary. Instead, these approaches can be used alongside traditional medicine to enhance overall wellness and support healing. For example, acupuncture or chiropractic care may be used to complement pain management strategies for a dog with arthritis, while herbal supplements might support liver function in a cat undergoing medication for hyperthyroidism.

As interest in holistic and alternative veterinary medicine grows, continuing education and training opportunities in these areas are expanding for veterinary professionals. Courses, workshops, and certifications allow veterinarians to gain expertise in specific modalities, ensuring that they can provide safe and effective care. Collaborating with specialists in holistic and alternative medicine can also enhance a veterinarian's ability to offer comprehensive treatment options.

The ethical considerations of holistic and alternative therapies are pivotal in ensuring that animal welfare remains the primary focus. Veterinarians must prioritize evidence-based practices and stay informed about the latest research to provide reliable and effective treatments. Balancing the benefits of these therapies with their limitations requires a thoughtful and informed approach.

Chapter 5

Surgical Skills and Techniques

Preparing for Surgery Sterilization and Safety

Surgical procedures in veterinary practice, whether routine or complex, demand meticulous preparation and adherence to safety protocols to ensure the well-being of animal patients. Preparing for surgery involves a series of steps that encompass pre-operative assessment, sterilization techniques, and safety measures, all designed to minimize risks and promote successful outcomes. This chapter delves into the comprehensive approach required for surgical preparation, providing practical guidance to veterinary professionals and students.

The pre-operative assessment is a critical component of surgical preparation, serving as the foundation for all subsequent steps. It begins with a thorough evaluation of the animal's medical history, including any previous surgeries, medications, and underlying health conditions. This information helps identify potential risk factors that may influence anesthesia or surgical outcomes. A physical examination is conducted to assess the animal's overall health, with particular attention to cardiovascular and respiratory function. Diagnostic tests, such as blood work and imaging, may be performed to gather additional data and ensure the animal is fit for surgery.

Informed consent is an essential aspect of the pre-operative process, involving clear communication with the pet owner about the nature of the surgery, potential risks, and expected outcomes. This dialogue fosters trust and ensures that the owner is fully aware of what to expect, both during and after the procedure. Providing written instructions and answering any questions can further support the owner in making informed decisions about their pet's care.

Sterilization is a cornerstone of surgical safety, aimed at preventing infections and ensuring a sterile environment. The process involves both the sterilization of surgical instruments and the maintenance of aseptic conditions in the operating room. Instruments are typically sterilized using autoclaves, which employ pressurized steam to eliminate microorganisms. Ensuring that all instruments are properly cleaned and sterilized is essential to prevent contamination and surgical site infections.

The operating room itself must be prepared to maintain sterility throughout the procedure. This involves cleaning and disinfecting surfaces, organizing equipment, and ensuring that all personnel follow strict aseptic protocols. Surgical attire, including gowns, gloves, masks, and caps, must be worn by all individuals in the operating room to prevent the introduction of contaminants. The use of sterile drapes and barriers further protects the surgical site from potential sources of infection.

Patient preparation is another critical aspect of surgical safety. The animal's fur is clipped and the skin is thoroughly cleaned and disinfected to reduce the risk of infection. Positioning the animal on the surgical table is done with care to ensure comfort and accessibility to the surgical site. Monitoring equipment, such as electrocardiograms, blood pressure monitors, and pulse oximeters, is connected to the patient to provide continuous data on physiological parameters throughout the procedure.

Anesthesia plays a pivotal role in surgical safety, requiring careful selection and administration of anesthetic agents. The choice of anesthesia depends on factors such as the animal's species, size, and health status, as well as the type of surgery being performed. Pre-anesthetic medications may be used to calm the animal and reduce anxiety, while the induction of anesthesia is typically achieved through injectable or inhalant agents. Monitoring the animal's vital signs during anesthesia is essential to ensure stability and detect any adverse reactions promptly.

Pain management is an integral part of surgical preparation and recovery, aimed at minimizing discomfort and promoting healing. Analgesics are administered pre-emptively and continued during and after the procedure to provide effective pain relief. A multimodal approach, using a combination of drugs with different mechanisms of action, enhances analgesic efficacy and reduces the need for higher doses of individual medications.

Post-operative care is crucial for ensuring a smooth recovery and minimizing complications. This involves monitoring the animal as they awaken from anesthesia, assessing their vital signs, and providing supportive care as needed. Instructions for post-operative care at home, including wound care, activity restrictions, and medication administration, are provided to the pet owner to ensure continuity of care. Follow-up appointments are scheduled to assess the animal's recovery and address any concerns that may arise.

Emergency protocols are an important aspect of surgical preparation, ensuring that the surgical team is ready to respond to any unexpected events. This includes having emergency drugs and equipment readily available, as well as a clear plan for managing complications such as bleeding, respiratory distress, or cardiac arrest. Regular training and drills can help the surgical team maintain readiness and confidence in handling emergencies.

Continuing education and professional development are essential for staying current with advances in surgical techniques, sterilization methods, and safety protocols. Attending workshops, conferences, and training sessions allows veterinary professionals to refine their skills and expand their knowledge, ultimately enhancing the quality of care provided to their animal patients.

Ethical considerations are integral to surgical preparation, emphasizing the veterinarian's responsibility to prioritize the welfare and comfort of their patients. This includes using evidence-based practices, minimizing pain and suffering, and ensuring that all surgical interventions are performed with the utmost care and precision.

Basic Surgical Procedures

Surgical procedures are an essential aspect of veterinary medicine, enabling practitioners to address a wide range of health issues and improve the quality of life for their animal patients. For beginners entering this field, understanding the fundamental techniques and principles of basic surgical procedures is crucial. This chapter focuses on the core aspects of performing surgical interventions, offering practical advice and insights to help build confidence and competence in novice veterinarians.

Before embarking on any surgical procedure, thorough preparation is paramount. This begins with a comprehensive understanding of the animal's anatomy, as familiarity with the structures involved is key to performing precise and effective surgery. Resources such as anatomical textbooks and 3D models can aid in visualizing the intricate details of various species, from the muscular and skeletal systems to the vascular and nervous networks.

Pre-operative planning involves selecting the appropriate surgical technique based on the condition being treated and the specific needs of the patient. Common basic surgical procedures include spays and neuters, wound repairs, and mass removals. Each procedure requires a tailored approach, taking into consideration factors such as the animal's size, age, and health status.

Surgical instruments are the tools of the trade, and knowing how to select and use them properly is essential. Scalpels, scissors, forceps, and retractors are among the basic instruments used in most procedures. Ensuring that instruments are sterilized and in good condition is critical to maintaining a sterile field and preventing infections. Mastery of techniques such as suturing is vital, as it directly impacts wound healing and cosmetic outcomes. Practicing on models or cadavers can help novice veterinarians develop dexterity and confidence in their suturing skills.

Anesthesia is a crucial component of any surgical procedure, providing pain relief and immobilization. Selecting the appropriate anesthetic protocol requires an understanding of the pharmacological properties of different agents and their effects on various species. Monitoring the animal's vital signs, such as heart rate, respiratory rate, and blood pressure, is necessary to ensure safety and stability throughout the procedure. Having a trained assistant to help monitor anesthesia and assist with surgical tasks can greatly enhance efficiency and safety.

The surgical environment must be meticulously prepared to maintain aseptic conditions. This involves cleaning and disinfecting the operating room, organizing instruments and supplies, and ensuring that all personnel adhere to strict sterile techniques. Wearing surgical attire, including gowns, gloves, masks, and caps, is mandatory to prevent contamination. A sterile field is created around the surgical site using drapes and barriers, minimizing the risk of infections.

Performing the surgery itself requires precision, patience, and adaptability. Following the planned surgical steps methodically ensures that each aspect of the procedure is addressed. However, unexpected challenges may arise, necessitating quick thinking and problem-solving skills. Staying calm and focused allows the surgeon to navigate complexities and make informed decisions.

Once the surgical procedure is completed, attention turns to closing the incision and ensuring proper wound healing. Careful suturing minimizes tension on the wound edges, reducing the risk of dehiscence and promoting optimal healing. Selecting the appropriate suture material and pattern is crucial, as different tissues require different techniques to ensure strength and support during the healing process.

Post-operative care is an integral part of the surgical journey, as it influences recovery and outcomes. Monitoring the animal as they emerge from anesthesia involves assessing vital signs, ensuring adequate pain management, and providing supportive care as needed. Clear, detailed instructions for post-operative care at home should be communicated to the pet owner, including guidelines for wound care, activity restrictions, and medication administration. Follow-up appointments are essential to monitor healing and address any complications that may arise.

Learning from each surgical experience is vital for growth and development as a veterinarian. Reflecting on the procedure, analyzing what went well, and identifying areas for improvement contribute to continuous skill enhancement. Seeking feedback from experienced colleagues and mentors can provide valuable insights and guidance.

Professional development and continuing education are essential for staying current with advances in surgical techniques and best practices. Attending workshops, conferences, and training sessions allows veterinarians to refine their skills and expand their knowledge, ultimately enhancing the quality of care provided to their animal patients.

Ethical considerations are at the heart of veterinary surgery, emphasizing the responsibility of veterinarians to prioritize the welfare and comfort of their patients. This includes using evidence-based practices, minimizing pain and suffering, and ensuring that all surgical interventions are performed with the utmost care and precision.

Post-Operative Care and Recovery

Post-operative care is a critical phase in the surgical journey of any animal patient, encompassing a range of practices aimed at ensuring a smooth recovery and minimizing complications. The period following surgery is when the body's healing processes are most active, and diligent care is essential to support these natural mechanisms. This chapter provides an in-depth look at the strategies and considerations involved in post-operative care and recovery, offering actionable advice for veterinary professionals and pet owners alike.

The immediate aftermath of surgery requires close monitoring as the animal emerges from anesthesia. This phase, known as the recovery period, is crucial for assessing the animal's vital signs and overall condition. Monitoring includes checking heart rate, respiratory rate, temperature, and blood pressure to ensure stability. The animal should be placed in a quiet, comfortable area, free from stressors that could hinder recovery. It's important to provide warmth, as anesthesia can lead to hypothermia. Blankets or heating pads can be used, but with caution to prevent burns.

Pain management is a cornerstone of post-operative care, as unmanaged pain can impede healing and affect the animal's well-being. A multimodal approach, utilizing a combination of analgesics, is often most effective. Opioids, NSAIDs, and local anesthetics may be administered, depending on the procedure and the patient's needs. Regular assessment of pain levels is necessary, as animals may not always exhibit overt signs of discomfort. Subtle changes in behavior, posture, or vocalization can indicate pain, requiring prompt attention and adjustment of the pain management plan.

Wound care is another essential aspect of post-operative recovery. Surgical incisions must be kept clean and dry to prevent infection. Veterinary professionals should instruct pet owners on how to care for the incision site at home, including cleaning techniques and signs of infection, such as redness, swelling, or discharge. An Elizabethan collar, or "cone," can be used to prevent the animal from licking or biting the wound, which could lead to complications. Regular check-ups allow veterinarians to monitor healing and intervene if issues arise.

Nutrition plays a pivotal role in recovery, as the body requires adequate nutrients to repair tissues and regain strength. Depending on the surgery and the animal's condition, dietary adjustments may be necessary. Easily digestible foods, rich in protein and essential nutrients, can support healing. Ensuring proper hydration is equally important, as dehydration can slow recovery and exacerbate post-operative complications. Veterinarians should provide guidance on feeding schedules and any dietary supplements that may aid recovery.

Activity restriction is often necessary to prevent strain on healing tissues and avoid complications. Veterinary professionals should provide clear instructions on how to limit the animal's activity, including leash walks and avoidance of jumping or running. Gradual reintroduction to normal activity levels, guided by the veterinarian, helps ensure a safe return to routine.

The emotional well-being of the animal is an often-overlooked component of post-operative care. Surgery and hospitalization can be stressful experiences, and providing a calm, reassuring environment is essential for recovery. Pet owners can offer comfort through gentle handling and spending quality time with their pets, fostering a sense of security and normalcy.

Communication between veterinarians and pet owners is vital throughout the recovery process. Providing clear, detailed instructions and addressing any concerns or questions ensures that pet owners are equipped to support their pet's recovery at home. Scheduled follow-up visits allow veterinarians to assess progress and make any necessary adjustments to the care plan.

Complications, while not common, can occur during the post-operative period, and being vigilant for signs is crucial. Infections, seromas, dehiscence, and adverse reactions to medications are some of the potential issues that may arise. Early detection and intervention can mitigate these complications and promote a successful recovery. Educating pet owners about the signs of complications and when to seek veterinary attention empowers them to act promptly if concerns arise.

Rehabilitation may be indicated for certain surgeries, especially those involving orthopedic or neurological issues. Physical therapy can enhance recovery by improving mobility, strength, and flexibility. Techniques such as hydrotherapy, passive range-of-motion exercises, and therapeutic ultrasound may be employed by trained professionals to support healing and restore function.

In some cases, alternative therapies can complement traditional post-operative care. Acupuncture, laser therapy, and massage are among the modalities that can aid recovery by reducing pain and inflammation and promoting circulation. Veterinarians should evaluate the suitability of these therapies for each individual patient and integrate them into a comprehensive care plan as appropriate.

Continual learning and professional development are essential for veterinary professionals to stay current with advancements in post-operative care. Engaging in workshops, conferences, and training sessions can enhance knowledge and skills, ultimately improving patient outcomes. Collaboration with specialists and colleagues also provides opportunities to share insights and best practices.

Ethical considerations underscore the responsibility of veterinarians to provide compassionate, evidence-based care that prioritizes the welfare of their patients. This commitment to excellence ensures that animals receive the highest standard of post-operative care, promoting healing, comfort, and a return to health.

Managing Surgical Complications

Managing surgical complications is an integral aspect of veterinary practice, demanding vigilance, skill, and adaptability from the veterinary team. Despite meticulous preparation and execution, complications can arise during or after surgical procedures, posing challenges that require prompt and effective responses. This chapter delves into the strategies and protocols necessary for identifying, addressing, and mitigating surgical complications, equipping veterinary professionals with the tools to navigate these situations successfully.

Complications can manifest in various forms, ranging from mild and easily managed to severe and life-threatening. Understanding the potential risks associated with different types of surgeries is the first step in preparing to manage complications. Common issues include hemorrhage, infection, anesthetic complications, and wound dehiscence. Each of these presents unique challenges and requires specific interventions to ensure the best possible outcomes for the patient.

Hemorrhage, or excessive bleeding, is a complication that can occur intra-operatively or post-operatively.

During surgery, careful hemostasis is crucial to prevent significant blood loss. Techniques such as ligation, cauterization, and the use of hemostatic agents can be employed to control bleeding. In the event of unexpected hemorrhage, maintaining a clear surgical field and quickly identifying the source of bleeding are essential steps. Post-operatively, veterinarians must monitor for signs of internal bleeding, such as pale mucous membranes, rapid heart rate, or abdominal distension. In cases of severe blood loss, fluid therapy or blood transfusions may be necessary to stabilize the patient.

Infection is another common complication that can arise from contamination of the surgical site. Preventive measures, such as strict aseptic technique and prophylactic antibiotics, are vital in minimizing this risk. However, if an infection does occur, prompt identification and treatment are paramount. Signs of infection include redness, swelling, heat, and discharge from the incision site. Cultures may be taken to identify the causative organism and guide antibiotic therapy. In some cases, surgical intervention may be required to drain abscesses or remove infected tissue.

Anesthetic complications, though relatively rare, can be serious and necessitate immediate attention. Monitoring the patient's vital signs throughout anesthesia is critical in detecting early signs of complications, such as hypotension, hypoventilation, or arrhythmias. Having emergency drugs and equipment readily available allows the veterinary team to respond swiftly to any adverse events. Post-anesthetic complications, such as prolonged recovery or aspiration pneumonia, require careful observation and supportive care to ensure patient safety.

Wound dehiscence, or the reopening of a surgical incision, can result from excessive tension on the wound, infection, or poor healing. Preventive measures include proper suture techniques, appropriate tension management, and post-operative activity restriction. If dehiscence occurs, assessing the extent of tissue separation is crucial to determine the appropriate course of action. Minor cases may be managed with local wound care and supportive bandaging, while more significant separations may necessitate surgical revision to reappose tissue layers.

The emotional impact of surgical complications on pet owners should not be underestimated. Open, empathetic communication is essential in maintaining trust and ensuring that owners are informed and involved in the decision-making process. Providing clear explanations of the situation, potential outcomes, and treatment options helps alleviate anxiety and fosters a collaborative approach to patient care.

Documentation is a fundamental aspect of managing surgical complications, ensuring that all observations, interventions, and communications are recorded accurately. Comprehensive records serve as valuable references for ongoing patient management and facilitate continuity of care among the veterinary team. They also provide critical information in the event of legal inquiries or ethical reviews.

Continuing education and training are vital for veterinary professionals to stay current with

advancements in surgical techniques and
complication management. Engaging in workshops,
seminars, and professional development courses
enhances knowledge and skills, ultimately improving
patient outcomes. Collaboration with specialists and
colleagues also provides opportunities to share
insights and best practices, fostering a culture of
continuous learning and improvement.

Ethical considerations are central to managing
surgical complications, underscoring the
responsibility of veterinarians to prioritize patient
welfare and provide evidence-based care. This
includes making informed decisions about the
potential benefits and risks of surgical interventions,
as well as engaging in open discussions about
prognosis and quality of life with pet owners.

Innovations in Veterinary Surgery

Innovations in veterinary surgery have revolutionized
the way practitioners approach animal health care,
offering new possibilities for treatment and recovery.
These advancements span a range of technologies and
techniques, enabling veterinarians to perform
surgeries with greater precision, reduced
invasiveness, and improved outcomes. The chapter
explores some of the most significant innovations
transforming veterinary surgery, providing insights
into how these developments can enhance practice
and patient care.

Minimally invasive surgery (MIS) has emerged as a
groundbreaking advancement, offering numerous
benefits over traditional open surgical techniques.

Laparoscopy and arthroscopy are two prominent forms of MIS that involve making small incisions through which specialized instruments and cameras are inserted. This approach minimizes trauma to surrounding tissues, leading to reduced pain, faster recovery times, and lower risk of complications. In veterinary practice, MIS is increasingly used for procedures such as spaying, gastrointestinal surgeries, and joint diagnostics, allowing animals to return to normal activities more quickly.

Laser surgery represents another innovative tool in veterinary medicine, utilizing focused light beams to make precise incisions, vaporize tissues, or coagulate blood vessels. Laser surgery reduces bleeding, swelling, and pain, making it ideal for delicate procedures such as tumor removal, soft palate resection, or ophthalmic surgeries. The precision of lasers also allows for targeted treatment of specific areas, minimizing damage to surrounding healthy tissues. As laser technology becomes more accessible, its applications in veterinary practice continue to expand, offering new solutions for a variety of conditions.

Advancements in imaging technology have significantly impacted surgical planning and execution, providing veterinarians with detailed insights into the anatomy and pathology of their patients. Computed tomography (CT) and magnetic resonance imaging (MRI) are invaluable tools that produce high-resolution, cross-sectional images, allowing for accurate diagnosis and surgical planning. These imaging modalities enable veterinarians to visualize complex structures, identify abnormalities, and tailor surgical approaches to each individual patient, ultimately enhancing surgical precision and outcomes.

3D printing technology has opened new avenues for innovation in veterinary surgery, offering the ability to create custom anatomical models, implants, and surgical guides. By converting imaging data into tangible 3D models, veterinarians can better understand complex cases, plan intricate surgeries, and practice procedures before operating on the patient. Custom implants and prosthetics can be designed to fit the unique anatomy of an animal, improving the success of reconstructive surgeries and enhancing quality of life. This technology not only aids in surgical preparation but also serves as an educational tool for veterinary professionals and students.

Regenerative medicine is a rapidly growing field that holds promise for revolutionizing surgical treatment and recovery. Stem cell therapy and platelet-rich plasma (PRP) are two regenerative approaches gaining traction in veterinary medicine. These treatments harness the body's natural healing processes to repair damaged tissues, reduce inflammation, and promote regeneration. In surgical settings, regenerative medicine can be used to enhance healing of wounds, tendons, and ligaments, offering new hope for conditions that may have been previously considered untreatable.

Robotic-assisted surgery represents the cutting edge of surgical innovation, providing veterinarians with enhanced dexterity and precision. While still in its early stages in veterinary medicine compared to human healthcare, robotic systems have the potential to perform complex procedures with minimal invasiveness. These systems offer advantages such as increased maneuverability, steadiness, and the ability to operate in confined spaces. As technology advances and becomes more cost-effective, robotic-assisted surgery is likely to become a more common feature in veterinary practice, expanding the possibilities for intricate surgical interventions.

Telemedicine and remote consultations have transformed the way veterinarians collaborate and seek expertise, particularly in surgical contexts. Through digital communication platforms, veterinarians can consult with specialists worldwide, receive guidance on complex cases, and access real-time support during surgeries. This connectivity enhances the quality of care by facilitating knowledge exchange and expanding access to specialized expertise, ultimately improving patient outcomes.

The integration of artificial intelligence (AI) in veterinary surgery is an emerging trend with the potential to revolutionize diagnostics, surgical planning, and decision-making. AI algorithms can analyze vast amounts of data to identify patterns, predict outcomes, and offer recommendations, assisting veterinarians in making informed decisions. In surgery, AI can enhance precision by guiding instrument placement, predicting complications, and optimizing surgical techniques. As AI technology continues to evolve, its applications in veterinary surgery are expected to grow, offering new tools for enhancing patient care.

Continuing education is essential for veterinary professionals to stay abreast of these innovations and incorporate them into practice effectively. Engaging in workshops, conferences, and training sessions allows veterinarians to explore new technologies, refine their skills, and expand their knowledge. Collaboration with experts and colleagues provides opportunities to share insights and best practices, fostering a culture of continuous learning and improvement.

Ethical considerations are paramount in the adoption and implementation of surgical innovations, underscoring the responsibility of veterinarians to prioritize patient welfare and provide evidence-based care. This includes evaluating the benefits and risks of new technologies, ensuring they are used appropriately, and engaging in open discussions with pet owners about treatment options and outcomes.

Chapter 6

Animal Nutrition and Well-being

Nutritional Needs of Different Animal Species

Understanding the nutritional needs of different animal species is a cornerstone of effective veterinary care, as nutrition plays a critical role in maintaining health, preventing disease, and supporting recovery. Each species has unique dietary requirements based on its physiology, environment, and life stage. This chapter provides insights into the diverse nutritional needs across species, offering practical guidance to veterinary professionals and pet owners in crafting appropriate diets.

Carnivores, such as cats and ferrets, have evolved to thrive on diets rich in animal protein and fat. Their digestive systems are adapted for processing meat, with a high requirement for specific amino acids like taurine, which is essential for heart and eye health. Unlike other animals, cats lack the ability to synthesize taurine, making it a critical dietary component. Additionally, they require arachidonic acid, a fatty acid found in animal tissues, as they cannot convert linoleic acid to arachidonic acid efficiently. When developing diets for carnivorous pets, it's important to ensure that these essential nutrients are adequately supplied to prevent deficiencies.

Herbivores, including rabbits, guinea pigs, and horses, have digestive systems uniquely adapted to process fibrous plant material. These animals rely on a diet high in fiber to maintain gastrointestinal health and function. Rabbits and guinea pigs, for example, require constant access to hay, which provides the necessary fiber for promoting gut motility and preventing dental issues. Vitamin C is another critical nutrient for guinea pigs, as they are unable to synthesize it on their own. Horses, with their large hindgut fermentation system, also need a high-fiber diet, supplemented with concentrates to meet their energy requirements, especially in working or performance animals.

Omnivores, such as dogs and pigs, have a more flexible dietary capacity, able to digest and utilize both plant and animal-based foods. While dogs can thrive on a variety of diets, balanced nutrition is crucial to meet their needs for protein, fats, carbohydrates, vitamins, and minerals. Life stage and activity level can influence dietary requirements, with puppies and active dogs needing more protein and calories than senior or sedentary dogs. Pigs, often kept as livestock or pets, require a balanced diet that supports growth, reproduction, and overall health. Providing a mix of grains, vegetables, and protein sources helps meet their nutritional demands.

Birds present another layer of complexity in nutritional planning. With a wide range of species, from parrots to finches, dietary needs can vary significantly. Many birds require a diet rich in seeds, fruits, and vegetables, but the proportions and specific types can differ. For instance, parrots need a mix of seeds, pellets, and fresh produce, while some species, like the lory, have a natural diet of nectar and fruits. Calcium is a vital nutrient for egg-laying birds to support shell formation and prevent deficiencies. Understanding the unique needs of each bird species is essential in preventing nutritional imbalances and related health issues.

Reptiles, encompassing a diverse group including turtles, snakes, and lizards, have dietary needs that reflect their natural habitats. Herbivorous reptiles, such as tortoises and iguanas, require diets rich in leafy greens, vegetables, and limited fruits. In contrast, carnivorous reptiles like snakes need a diet of whole prey to mimic their natural feeding habits. Omnivores, such as some species of lizards, benefit from a varied diet of insects, fruits, and vegetables. Providing appropriate calcium and vitamin D3 supplementation is crucial for reptiles to prevent metabolic bone disease, a common issue in captive environments.

Fish, whether freshwater or marine, also have unique nutritional requirements based on species and habitat. Protein is a primary component of most fish diets, but the source and balance of other nutrients can vary. For instance, herbivorous fish need more plant material in their diet, while carnivorous species require more animal-based protein. The availability of commercial fish foods tailored to specific species has made it easier to meet the nutritional needs of captive fish, yet understanding the natural diet remains key to preventing deficiencies and supporting health.

Life stage and health status further influence nutritional needs across all species. Young, growing animals have higher energy and protein demands to support development, while pregnant or lactating females require increased nutrients to nourish their offspring. Senior animals may benefit from diets lower in calories but rich in antioxidants to support aging bodies. Animals with medical conditions, such as kidney disease or diabetes, often require specialized diets to manage their health effectively.

Environmental factors also play a role in shaping dietary requirements. Animals living in colder climates may need more energy-dense diets to maintain body temperature, while those in warmer climates might have different hydration needs. Access to natural sunlight, which influences vitamin D synthesis, can affect dietary requirements for calcium and phosphorus, particularly in reptiles and birds.

Creating balanced diets requires a comprehensive understanding of each species' nutritional needs, dietary habits, and health considerations. Veterinary professionals play a crucial role in guiding pet owners and animal caregivers in selecting appropriate commercial diets or formulating homemade diets that meet all nutritional requirements. Regular assessments and adjustments to diets can help address changing needs and prevent nutritional deficiencies or excesses.

Education and communication are key in ensuring that pet owners understand the importance of proper nutrition and its impact on their animals' health. Providing resources, such as dietary guidelines and feeding schedules, empowers owners to make informed decisions and fosters a collaborative approach to care. Encouraging owners to observe and report changes in their pets' behavior or health can help identify potential nutritional issues early.

Continuous learning is essential for veterinary professionals to stay updated on advancements in nutritional science and dietary formulations. Engaging in workshops, seminars, and professional development courses enhances knowledge and skills, ultimately improving the quality of care provided to animal patients. Collaborating with nutritionists and specialists also provides opportunities to share insights and best practices, fostering a culture of continuous improvement.

Ethical considerations are integral to nutritional planning, emphasizing the responsibility of veterinarians to prioritize animal welfare and provide evidence-based dietary recommendations. This includes evaluating the benefits and risks of different feeding approaches, ensuring diets are balanced and appropriate, and engaging in open discussions with pet owners about nutrition and health.

The Role of Diet in Disease Prevention and Recovery

Diet is a cornerstone of health, serving as both a preventive measure and a therapeutic tool in the management of diseases across various animal species. Understanding the intricate relationship between nutrition and disease not only aids in prevention but also supports recovery, enhancing the overall well-being of animals. This chapter delves into the vital role diet plays in both preventing disease and aiding recovery, offering practical guidance for veterinary professionals and pet owners.

Prevention begins with a balanced diet that meets the specific nutritional needs of each animal species. Proper nutrition supports the immune system, helping to ward off infections and chronic diseases. An optimal balance of macronutrients—proteins, fats, and carbohydrates—along with essential vitamins and minerals, forms the foundation of a healthy diet. These nutrients work synergistically to maintain physiological functions, repair tissues, and regulate metabolism.

Antioxidants, found abundantly in fruits and vegetables, play a crucial role in disease prevention. They combat oxidative stress by neutralizing free radicals, which are unstable molecules that can damage cells and contribute to aging and various diseases. Incorporating antioxidant-rich foods into an animal's diet can reduce the risk of conditions such as cancer, cardiovascular disease, and inflammatory disorders. For example, blueberries and carrots are excellent sources of antioxidants that can be included in the diets of dogs and birds.

Fatty acids, particularly omega-3s and omega-6s, are essential components of a disease-preventive diet. These healthy fats contribute to maintaining cell membrane integrity, reducing inflammation, and supporting brain and heart health. Fish oil, flaxseed, and chia seeds are natural sources of omega-3 fatty acids that can be beneficial for dogs, cats, and even some herbivorous species when used appropriately. Balancing omega-3 and omega-6 fatty acids is key to optimizing their anti-inflammatory benefits.

Fiber, often overlooked, is indispensable for maintaining digestive health and preventing diseases such as obesity, diabetes, and certain types of cancer. High-fiber diets support healthy gut flora, improve bowel movements, and regulate blood sugar levels. Herbivorous animals, like rabbits and guinea pigs, rely heavily on fiber-rich diets, while omnivores and carnivores can benefit from appropriate fiber inclusion to maintain intestinal health.

When disease strikes, nutrition becomes a critical component of the recovery process. Certain conditions, such as renal disease, diabetes, and gastrointestinal disorders, necessitate dietary modifications to manage symptoms and support healing. For instance, animals with kidney disease may require diets low in phosphorus and protein to reduce the burden on the kidneys and slow disease progression. Specialized renal diets are formulated to meet these needs, promoting improved quality of life for affected animals.

In cases of diabetes, controlling carbohydrate intake is crucial to managing blood sugar levels. Diets rich in complex carbohydrates and fiber can help stabilize glucose levels, reducing the risk of complications. Additionally, weight management plays a significant role in diabetes care, as obesity can exacerbate insulin resistance. Veterinary professionals must work closely with pet owners to develop tailored feeding plans that address the individual needs of diabetic animals.

Gastrointestinal disorders, such as inflammatory bowel disease (IBD) or pancreatitis, often require specific dietary adjustments to reduce inflammation and support digestion. Easily digestible diets, low in fat and high in digestible protein, can alleviate symptoms and promote healing. In some cases, novel protein or hypoallergenic diets are necessary to identify and eliminate dietary triggers. Careful monitoring and adjustments are essential to ensure the diet meets the animal's nutritional requirements without exacerbating the condition.

The role of nutrition in cancer care is multifaceted, focusing on supporting the immune system, maintaining body weight, and managing side effects of treatment. Diets for animals with cancer often emphasize high-quality protein, healthy fats, and antioxidants to support immune function and tissue repair. Omega-3 fatty acids can help reduce inflammation and inhibit tumor growth, while antioxidants combat oxidative stress induced by cancer and its treatment. Ensuring adequate caloric intake is vital, as cancer and its therapies can lead to weight loss and muscle wasting.

Rehabilitation from surgery or injury also benefits significantly from nutritional support. Protein is a key nutrient in this context, providing the building blocks necessary for tissue repair and recovery. Increasing protein intake during the recovery phase can accelerate healing and restore strength. Additionally, vitamins and minerals such as vitamin C, zinc, and magnesium play crucial roles in collagen synthesis and wound healing, making them important components of post-operative diets.

Hydration, often underestimated, is a fundamental aspect of both disease prevention and recovery. Adequate water intake supports kidney function, aids digestion, and helps regulate body temperature.

Ensuring animals have constant access to fresh, clean water is essential, particularly for those with urinary or metabolic conditions where fluid balance is critical.

Education is paramount in empowering pet owners to make informed decisions about their animals' diets. Veterinary professionals can provide valuable resources, such as feeding guidelines and nutritional counseling, to help owners understand the impact of diet on health. Encouraging owners to observe their pets' responses to dietary changes and report any concerns can facilitate early intervention and adaptation of feeding plans.

Continuous professional development is crucial for veterinarians to stay informed about the latest research and advancements in animal nutrition. Engaging in workshops, seminars, and collaborations with nutritionists enhances knowledge and skills, allowing veterinarians to provide evidence-based dietary recommendations tailored to individual animal needs.

Ethical considerations underscore the responsibility of veterinarians to prioritize the welfare of their patients through appropriate nutritional care. This includes evaluating the benefits and risks of dietary interventions, ensuring diets are balanced and evidence-based, and engaging in open discussions with pet owners about nutrition and health.

Managing Obesity and Metabolic Disorders

Obesity and metabolic disorders in animals present significant challenges for veterinary professionals and pet owners alike. As lifestyles change and animals increasingly adapt to human environments, the prevalence of these conditions has risen, necessitating effective management strategies. Understanding the underlying causes, health implications, and treatment approaches is crucial for tackling these issues and promoting healthier lives for affected animals.

Obesity is characterized by excessive body fat accumulation, resulting from an imbalance between caloric intake and energy expenditure. Various factors contribute to this imbalance, including genetics, diet, physical activity, and environmental influences. Certain breeds, such as Labrador Retrievers and Beagles, may have a genetic predisposition to weight gain, making them more susceptible to obesity. However, lifestyle factors often play a more significant role, with overfeeding and lack of exercise being primary contributors.

The health implications of obesity are profound, affecting nearly every system in the body. Overweight animals face an increased risk of developing conditions such as arthritis, cardiovascular disease, diabetes, and respiratory issues. Additionally, obesity can reduce life expectancy and diminish the quality of life, as excess weight places strain on joints and organs. Recognizing the impact of obesity on overall health underscores the importance of implementing preventive and management measures.

Metabolic disorders, often intertwined with obesity, encompass a range of conditions that affect the body's ability to process and utilize nutrients efficiently. Diabetes mellitus is one of the most common metabolic disorders in animals, characterized by impaired insulin production or function, leading to elevated blood glucose levels. Other metabolic disorders include hypothyroidism, Cushing's disease, and hyperlipidemia, each with its own set of clinical manifestations and management requirements.

Effective management of obesity and metabolic disorders begins with accurate diagnosis and assessment. Veterinary professionals utilize tools such as body condition scoring (BCS) and body weight measurements to evaluate an animal's weight status. BCS involves visual and tactile assessment of the animal's body fat, providing a standardized method for determining whether an animal is underweight, ideal, or overweight. Regular monitoring of BCS and body weight is essential for tracking progress and making necessary adjustments to treatment plans.

Dietary modification is a cornerstone of managing obesity and metabolic disorders. Transitioning to a balanced, calorie-controlled diet is critical for weight loss and metabolic regulation. Veterinary professionals should collaborate with pet owners to develop customized feeding plans that consider the animal's age, breed, activity level, and health status. Portion control, along with the selection of appropriate low-calorie or prescription diets, helps achieve and maintain a healthy weight. Additionally, educating pet owners about the importance of avoiding table scraps and excessive treats can prevent overfeeding and promote adherence to dietary recommendations.

Exercise and physical activity play pivotal roles in weight management and metabolic health. Encouraging regular exercise helps increase energy expenditure, promote muscle mass development, and improve overall fitness. For dogs, activities such as walking, running, and playing fetch are excellent ways to enhance physical activity. Cats, though often more sedentary, can benefit from interactive play with toys and climbing structures to stimulate movement. Tailoring exercise routines to the individual animal's capabilities and preferences ensures sustainability and effectiveness.

When addressing metabolic disorders, specific interventions may be required based on the underlying condition. For instance, managing diabetes mellitus involves regulating blood glucose levels through dietary adjustments, insulin therapy, and routine monitoring. Consistent feeding schedules, with controlled carbohydrate intake, help stabilize glucose levels. Insulin administration, tailored to the animal's needs, is often necessary for diabetic management, requiring pet owners to be well-informed and comfortable with the process.

Hypothyroidism, characterized by reduced thyroid hormone production, often leads to weight gain and lethargy. Treatment typically involves hormone replacement therapy, which restores normal metabolic function and alleviates symptoms. Regular monitoring of thyroid hormone levels ensures appropriate dosing and management.

Cushing's disease, resulting from excessive cortisol production, can contribute to obesity and metabolic disturbances. Treatment options may include medication to reduce cortisol levels or surgical intervention to remove the source of excess hormone production. Close monitoring and adjustment of treatment plans are essential to achieve optimal outcomes.

Hyperlipidemia, characterized by elevated blood lipid levels, requires dietary management to reduce fat intake and promote lipid metabolism. Low-fat diets, combined with regular exercise, help lower lipid levels and prevent complications such as pancreatitis or cardiovascular disease. In some cases, medication may be prescribed to aid in lipid regulation.

Communication and education are critical components of successful management. Veterinary professionals should provide pet owners with comprehensive information about the health risks associated with obesity and metabolic disorders, emphasizing the importance of adherence to treatment plans. Regular follow-up appointments allow for progress evaluation, troubleshooting, and ongoing support, fostering a collaborative approach to care.

Preventive measures are equally vital in addressing obesity and metabolic disorders. Promoting balanced nutrition, portion control, and regular exercise from an early age can help prevent the onset of these conditions. Encouraging pet owners to monitor their animals' weight and body condition regularly can facilitate early detection and intervention, reducing the risk of complications.

Continuous professional development enables veterinarians to stay informed about the latest research and advancements in managing obesity and metabolic disorders. Engaging in workshops, seminars, and collaborations with specialists enhances knowledge and skills, allowing for evidence-based recommendations tailored to individual animal needs.

Ethical considerations are central to managing obesity and metabolic disorders, underscoring the responsibility of veterinarians to prioritize patient welfare and provide evidence-based care. This includes evaluating the benefits and risks of treatment interventions, ensuring diets and exercise plans are safe and appropriate, and engaging in open discussions with pet owners about health and well-being.

Evaluating Commercial and Homemade Diets

Choosing the right diet for animals is a vital aspect of their health and well-being. With a plethora of commercial options and the growing popularity of homemade diets, making informed decisions requires a thorough evaluation of both approaches. Understanding the benefits and challenges of each helps ensure that animals receive balanced, nutritious meals tailored to their needs.

Commercial diets dominate the pet food market, offering convenience and a wide range of options tailored to different species, life stages, and health conditions. These diets are typically formulated to meet established nutritional guidelines, ensuring they provide essential nutrients in appropriate proportions. Complete and balanced commercial diets are designed to cover all dietary needs without the need for additional supplements, making them a practical choice for many pet owners.

One of the primary advantages of commercial diets is consistency. Each batch is manufactured to provide the same nutrient profile, reducing the risk of nutritional imbalances. This consistency is particularly important for animals with specific dietary requirements or health conditions, where precise nutrient intake is crucial. Additionally, commercial diets undergo rigorous testing and quality control measures to ensure safety and compliance with regulatory standards.

However, not all commercial diets are created equal. The quality of ingredients and the manufacturing process can vary significantly between brands and product lines. When evaluating commercial diets, it's essential to scrutinize the ingredient list and nutritional information. Look for high-quality protein sources, such as chicken, beef, or fish, listed as primary ingredients, and avoid products with excessive fillers like corn or soy. Evaluating the presence of artificial additives, colors, and preservatives is also critical, as these can affect the overall health of the animal.

Understanding the nutritional needs of the specific animal and matching them with the diet's profile is key to selecting the right commercial product. Consulting with a veterinarian can provide valuable insights into choosing a diet that aligns with the animal's health status, lifestyle, and preferences. Regular monitoring of the animal's health and condition can also help determine if the chosen diet is meeting their needs or if adjustments are necessary.

Homemade diets offer an alternative approach, allowing pet owners to have complete control over the ingredients and preparation methods. This is particularly appealing to those who prefer natural or organic ingredients, or whose pets have allergies or sensitivities to certain commercial diet components. Homemade diets can be tailored to cater to specific preferences and health requirements, offering a personalized approach to nutrition.

Crafting a balanced homemade diet, however, requires careful planning and knowledge of nutritional requirements. It is not merely about cooking meals for animals; it involves ensuring that all essential nutrients—proteins, fats, carbohydrates, vitamins, and minerals—are provided in the correct ratios. Nutritional deficiencies or imbalances can lead to serious health issues, making it imperative to consult with a veterinary nutritionist when developing a homemade diet plan.

One common challenge with homemade diets is ensuring adequate micronutrient intake. Vitamins and minerals, though required in small amounts, are vital for various physiological functions. Ingredients such as meat, grains, and vegetables may not inherently provide all necessary nutrients, requiring the addition of supplements to achieve a balanced meal. For instance, calcium and phosphorus ratios must be carefully managed, especially in growing animals, to support bone development and prevent skeletal issues.

Attention to food safety is crucial when preparing homemade diets. Raw or undercooked foods can harbor pathogens like Salmonella or E. coli, posing health risks to both animals and humans. Proper handling, storage, and preparation techniques are essential to minimize contamination and ensure the safety of homemade meals. Cooking certain ingredients can enhance digestibility and nutrient availability, making them safer and more beneficial.

Cost is another factor to consider when evaluating commercial versus homemade diets. While high-quality commercial diets may carry a higher price tag, they often require less preparation time and reduce the need for additional supplements. Homemade diets, while potentially more economical, demand time and effort to source ingredients, prepare meals, and ensure nutritional adequacy. Balancing time, cost, and nutritional value is key to determining the most suitable option for each animal and owner.

Transitioning between diets, whether commercial to homemade or vice versa, should be done gradually to allow the animal's digestive system to adjust. Sudden changes in diet can lead to gastrointestinal upset, stressing the importance of a slow and steady introduction of new foods. Monitoring the animal's response during this transition period helps identify any adverse reactions or preferences, guiding further dietary adjustments.

Education and communication play critical roles in guiding pet owners through the process of selecting and evaluating diets. Veterinary professionals can provide resources, such as dietary guidelines and sample recipes, to assist in making informed decisions. Encouraging pet owners to observe their animals' health and behavior helps identify potential dietary issues and facilitates early intervention.

Continuous professional development is essential for veterinarians to stay informed about the latest research and trends in animal nutrition. Engaging in workshops, seminars, and collaborations with nutritionists enhances knowledge and skills, enabling veterinarians to offer evidence-based recommendations tailored to individual animal needs.

Ethical considerations underscore the responsibility of veterinarians to prioritize animal welfare through appropriate nutritional guidance. This includes evaluating the benefits and risks of different dietary approaches, ensuring diets are balanced and safe, and engaging in open discussions with pet owners about nutrition and health.

Behavioral Enrichment and Mental Health

Animals thrive in environments that engage their minds and bodies. Behavioral enrichment is a powerful tool for enhancing mental health and overall well-being, promoting natural behaviors, and reducing stress. Understanding and implementing enrichment strategies can significantly improve the quality of life for animals in domestic, farm, and zoological settings, offering a window into their complex needs and capacities.

In the wild, animals are constantly challenged by their environments, which require them to engage in activities such as foraging, hunting, socializing, and exploring. These activities provide mental stimulation and keep animals physically active, playing a crucial role in their mental health. In contrast, animals in captivity or domestic settings often face limited opportunities to express these natural behaviors, leading to boredom, frustration, and stress, which can manifest as behavioral issues or health problems.

Behavioral enrichment seeks to bridge this gap by introducing elements that stimulate the senses, encourage problem-solving, and promote active engagement. These enrichment activities can take many forms, from simple toys and puzzles to complex environmental modifications that mimic natural habitats. The key is to tailor enrichment to the specific needs and preferences of each species and individual, ensuring it effectively meets their mental and physical requirements.

For domestic pets like dogs and cats, enrichment can be integrated into daily routines through interactive play, training exercises, and environmental modifications. Dogs, with their keen sense of smell and love for exploration, benefit from activities that challenge their olfactory abilities, such as scent trails or puzzle feeders. These activities not only provide mental stimulation but also mimic the foraging behavior of their wild ancestors. Similarly, cats enjoy engaging their hunting instincts through toys that mimic prey, such as feather wands or laser pointers, providing both exercise and cognitive engagement.

Social animals, such as parrots and rabbits, thrive on interaction and companionship, making social enrichment vital. For parrots, providing opportunities for socialization with humans or other birds can prevent loneliness and associated behavioral issues. Encouraging natural behaviors like foraging through treat-dispensing toys or hiding food around their environment can also stimulate their minds and reduce stress. Rabbits, often kept in pairs or groups, require ample space to explore and engage in social activities. Providing tunnels, platforms, and chewable toys can enrich their environment and promote natural behaviors.

In zoological settings, where animals are often housed in enclosures, enrichment is critical for maintaining mental health and reducing stereotypic behaviors. Zookeepers and animal care professionals employ a variety of techniques to simulate natural habitats and encourage species-specific behaviors. For example, primates may be provided with climbing structures, ropes, and puzzle feeders to promote physical activity and cognitive engagement. Elephants benefit from enrichment that encourages natural foraging and social behaviors, such as scattering food throughout their enclosures or providing large objects for manipulation.

Farm animals, too, require enrichment to prevent boredom and enhance welfare. Pigs, known for their intelligence, enjoy rooting and exploring, which can be facilitated by providing straw bedding and interactive feeders. Chickens benefit from opportunities to peck and scratch, achievable through hanging food items or scattering grains. These activities not only improve mental health but also lead to better physical health and productivity.

Implementing effective enrichment strategies requires an understanding of the natural history and behavioral needs of each species. Observing animals and assessing their responses to different enrichment activities can guide adjustments and improvements, ensuring that enrichment remains effective and engaging. Regularly changing and rotating enrichment items prevents habituation, keeping animals interested and mentally stimulated.

Enrichment is not only about providing physical objects or activities but also about creating environments that support natural behaviors. This can include designing spaces that allow for exploration, nesting, and social interaction, as well as ensuring access to natural elements like sunlight, water, and vegetation. These environmental modifications can have profound effects on mental health, reducing stress and promoting a sense of well-being.

The role of enrichment extends beyond individual animal welfare, impacting overall animal management and care. Animals that are mentally and physically stimulated are less likely to exhibit problem behaviors, reducing the need for interventions and improving the human-animal bond. Enrichment also enhances the educational and conservation value of zoological and farm settings by promoting natural behaviors and providing visitors with insights into the lives of animals.

Education and communication are essential in promoting the importance of enrichment and mental health. Veterinary professionals, animal caretakers, and pet owners can benefit from resources and training that highlight effective enrichment strategies and their impact on well-being. Encouraging collaboration and information-sharing among these groups fosters a culture of continuous improvement and innovation in animal care.

Ethical considerations are central to enrichment practices, emphasizing the responsibility to prioritize animal welfare and provide environments that support mental and physical health. This includes evaluating the benefits and potential risks of enrichment activities, ensuring they are safe and appropriate, and engaging in open discussions about the role of enrichment in animal management.